EMERALD GREENS

THE ESSENTIAL GUIDE TO
HOLIDAY GOLF IN IRELAND

ROISIN MCAULEY

First published in 2000
by The Appletree Press Ltd
The Old Potato Station
14 Howard Street South
Belfast BT7 1AP

Tel: + 44 (0) 28 90 243074
Fax: + 44 (0) 28 90 246756
E-mail: reception@appletree.ie
Web Site: www.appletree.ie

Text © Roisin McAuley, 2000

Emerald Greens – The Essential Guide to Holiday Golf in Ireland

A Catalogue for this book is available from the British Library

ISBN 0-86281-786-2

9 8 7 6 5 4 3 2 1

Acknowledgements

I would like to thank my husband, Richard Lee, who played many courses with me and was an uncomplaining golf widower the rest of the time; my mother, who provided a base for me in Ireland; Una Grant, Anne Mac Mahon, Maura Mac Mahon, Eleanor Devine, Jake Lee, Tony McAuley, Barbara Edwards, and Jean Thaxter – who turned out in all weathers to play the courses with me and give me the benefit of their experience; and the club secretaries, managers, professionals and greenkeepers who made playing the golf courses in *Emerald Greens* such an enjoyable experience.

The publisher wishes to thank:

Bord Fáilte - Irish Tourist Board for permission to publish photographs on pages 17, 20, 36, 44-45, 52-53, 56-57, 76, 80-81, 88, 93, 96, 100, 108, 125, 128-129, 137 and 141.

The Northern Ireland Tourist Board for permission to publish photographs on pages 12, 153, 157, 161, 165 and 169.

Liam White for permission to publish photographs on pages 32-33, 56-57, 64-65, 69, 116-117 and 121.

The Royal County Down Golf Club for permission to publish the photograph on page 148.

CONTENTS

FOREWORD   5

INTRODUCTION   6

THE GLENS OF ANTRIM AND THE CAUSEWAY COAST   8

DERRY CITY AND INISHOWEN   22

NORTH AND SOUTH DONEGAL   34

ROSSES POINT TO ERRIS HEAD   50

GALWAY CITY AND CONNEMARA   62

THE SOUTH WEST   72

NORTH EAST CORK   90

WATERFORD AND THE HOOK   102

WICKLOW   112

THE CENTRE OF IRELAND   124

BOYNE VALLEY   134

THE MOUNTAINS OF MOURNE   144

STRANGFORD LOUGH AND LECALE   154

TYRONE   164

MAP OF IRELAND   172

INDEX OF GOLF COURSES   174

Ireland is a great country for golfers. It has more courses per head of population than any other country in the world, so there's plenty of room for visitors. It has 40% of all the links in the world. The Golfing Union of Ireland, founded in 1891, is the oldest national golfing union. All the four provinces, Ulster, Munster, Leinster and Connacht boast a variety of courses - seaside, cliff-top, heath and parkland, old and new - within easy reach of one another.

Spend some time off the golf course too. Go sightseeing. Explore Ireland's rich history and culture. There's good music and conversation around every corner - the combination we call "good craic".

Northern Ireland is one of the best-kept secrets in golf. Come and be charmed by the quality of the courses, the beauty and tranquillity of the scenery, and the delights waiting to be discovered - not least in my home county, Tyrone.

If you know anything at all about the Irish you won't be surprised by the warm welcome we extend to visitors. And you don't even have to play golf.

Darren Clarke

"Golf widow: a woman whose husband spends much of his
spare time playing golf." (OED)

To avoid becoming a golf widow, the author took up the game and was initially baffled by the rules, the Stableford system, and the checked trousers worn by both sexes. Because Irish golf courses are set in stunning scenery, lost balls turn up in clumps of wild pansies, and hot whiskey tastes even more wonderful after 18 holes in the wind and rain, she persevered. She is now fanatical about golf and plays her way round a selection of Irish courses every night instead of counting sheep.

"If you can't beat 'em, join 'em." (Anon)

Golf experts put three Irish courses – Royal County Down, Ballybunion and Royal Portrush – in the world's top ten courses. Waterville, Portstewart and The European Club are in the world's top two hundred and fifty. But with fame have come bus tours, higher green fees and the necessity to book tee times months in advance. Some of Ireland's best courses have become places of pilgrimage for packaged tours. From late spring to early autumn, fourballs tee off at ten-minute intervals and marshalls monitor play on world-famous courses such as Ballybunion. These are a glorious challenge. But they are not what this book is principally about.

Ireland still conceals many of its golfing treasures. Visitors who set out in a leisurely way to explore Ireland's history, landscape, culture and people, will find a little-known gem of a golf course (or two or three or more) along the road. This book is for them. It is a guide to golf in great locations and is not intended for the scalp-hunter. Some world-famous courses – Royal County Down, Waterville and The European Club – are included because they can be played for less than £50 at off-peak times.

The attractions beyond the 18th green lie along routes connecting the golf courses in each area. The tourist information offices (addresses and telephone numbers are included) will tell you about many more things to do and see, where to stay, where to eat and where to shop.

In Ireland, the early bird catches the worm. Irish golfers, in general, don't turn out at the crack of dawn, or even for a few hours after it. You will find several courses have a special "early bird" green fee which includes breakfast or a snack. You then have the rest of the day to sightsee. Some courses give reductions for late afternoon tee times, some give reductions to husbands and wives playing together. Mid-week is always quieter than weekends. Book as far in advance as possible if you want to be sure of a weekend tee-time.

It is worth asking for dates of open days and open weeks when you can play at bargain rates in club competitions. You will need to produce your handicap certificate for these.

Some courses measure in metres, some in yards, some in both. The guide gives the total length of each course, in metres and yards, from the back tees. Don't be intimidated by what seem like very long courses. These usually have a selection of forward tees.

Facilities vary from club to club and from season to season. Some clubs have shops selling a wide range of equipment, clothing and accessories. Others just keep a stock of golf balls and tees behind the bar or in the office. Some clubs don't even have a bar. Others have a bar and a restaurant. You could be paying your green fees and changing in a luxurious clubhouse with visitors' lockers and hot showers, or changing your shoes in the carpark and posting your fees in an honesty box. The weather is unpredictable. Bring your wet-weather gear. The only constants are the excellence of the courses selected, the beauty of the scenery and the warmth of the welcome. Happy golfing.

"Don't hurry. Don't worry. You're only here on a
short visit. So don't forget to stop and smell the roses"
(Walter Hagen)

Key to maps: Golf Courses
△ Attractions

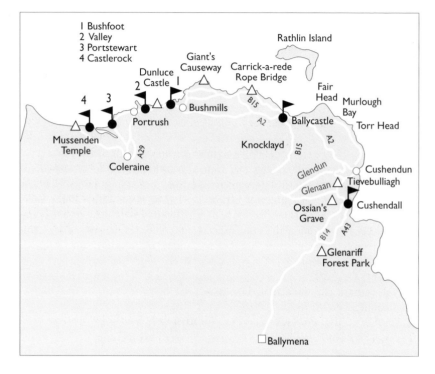

1 Bushfoot
2 Valley
3 Portstewart
4 Castlerock

Rathlin Island

Giant's
Causeway

Dunluce
Castle

Carrick-a-rede
Rope Bridge

Fair
Head

Murlough
Bay

Bushmills

Ballycastle

Torr Head

Portrush

Mussenden
Temple

Knocklayd

Coleraine

Cushendun

Glendun

Tievebulliagh

Glenaan

Cushendall

Ossian's
Grave

Glenariff
Forest Park

Ballymena

(Golf Courses: Cushendall, Ballycastle, Bushfoot, Portrush, Portstewart and Castlerock)

Distances: Cushendall to Ballycastle 25km/16miles; Ballycastle to Bushmills 21km/13miles; Bushmills to Castlerock 30km/18miles.

The nine Glens of Antrim cut inland from the lovely corniche coast road between Glenarm and the Giant's Causeway. From the Causeway to Castlerock, in County Derry, the coastal plains of the River Bush and the River Bann spread out towards cliffs of white chalk and dark basalt, rocky headlands, small harbours and sweeping strands. The Giant's Causeway has been a tourist attraction since 1693 when the Royal Geographical Society published a description of it. The

Causeway was formed by lava which erupted through the earth's crust some 60 million years ago and cooled slowly enough to form the familiar polygonal columns and colonnades. The drive around the north Antrim coast is one of the most famous scenic routes in Europe.

CUSHENDALL
9 holes – par 66 (4386metres/4873yards)
Shore Road, Cushendall.
Green Fees: £13 Monday to Friday, £18 weekends and bank holidays.
Telephone: 028 217 71318

The course lies between the village of Cushendall and the pretty pebble beach at the shore. The River Dall meanders along Shore Street and winds its way across the course to enter the sea under an arched wooden bridge beside the first tee. It flows along the 1st fairway and the back of the 1st and 8th greens. There are three tee-shots across the river. The 2nd/11th is a long par 3 (162metres/177yards) across the river to an elevated green. The 5th a pitch up to the green on the opposite bank. The 9th/18th – the longest hole on the course at 358metres/392yards – takes you across the river again and back to the clubhouse. There are no par 5s but the river lends charm and interest and you can go out of bounds on every hole. There are lovely views of Cushendall Bay, Garron Point, Lurigethean Mountain and, on fine days, the Mull of Kintyre, Sanda and Ailsa Craig.

BALLYCASTLE
18 holes – par 71 (5066metres/5629yards)
At the junction of the A2 and A44 in Ballycastle.
Green Fees: £20 weekdays, £28 weekends and bank holidays, £70 weekly.
Telephone: 028 207 62536

Ballycastle is an historic course in more than one sense. In November 1891, together with eight other clubs, it founded the Golfing Union of Ireland and gained its place in golfing history. It is also part of local history. On the course itself lie the ruins of Bonamargy Friary, founded by Rory McQuillan in 1500. The friary was built inside an earlier earthen enclosure. The course incorporates three different styles of golf course – meadowland, links and cliff-top. Although there is a sequence of six par 4s on the front nine, they are played over different terrain. You cross the Cushendall Road to play the first five holes around the ruins of the friary in a triangle of meadowland bordered by the Margy and Carey rivers, and the road. The 1st runs back up the Margy towards Glenshesk. (The Margy, which is joined by the Carey at the back of the 1st green is associated with the legendary Children of Lir who were changed into swans and condemned to roam the waters of Ireland for 900 years.) The 5th tee is on raised ground said to have been the citadel of the Queen of ancient Dalriada. Ahead, out to sea, is

Rathlin Island. Cross back over the road to play five links holes. The 6th and 7th run along the beach. (A big hitter might drive the 6th green.) The 9th requires a blind shot to the green up in a coll. At the back of the green is a sheer drop to a road running along the shore. The 10th (par 3) is uphill again over a steep bank of gorse to high ground on the top of a cliff. The next seven holes are played on this high ground with wonderful views of Ballycastle town, Kenbane Head, Fairhead, and Rathlin Island with its high white cliffs and three lighthouses. The coast of Scotland is often visible beyond. The wind is nearly always in the reckoning up here. On the 14th (a long par 4) there are also fine views of Knocklayde (Cnoc Leithid – "Hill of the Slope") and Glenshesk (Gleann Seisc – "Barren Glen") to your left. The 17th takes you back down the cliff for a finish on the links land.

BUSHFOOT

9 holes – par 70 (5876yards/5288metres)
Take the first turning for Portballintrae on the coast road after Bushmills.
The golf course is signposted off this road.
Green Fees: £15 weekdays, £20 weekends and bank holidays.
Telephone: 028 207 31317

Bushfoot as its name suggests, is beautifully sited where the River Bush flows into the sea at a strip of beach backed by high dunes. The nine holes are laid out on land separated by the river from sand dunes to the north and farmland to the east. It is not entirely links land. Three holes are played over parkland. There is a magnificent view from the first, elevated men's tee. The quiet river flows along the back of the dunes, the coast rises to the headland at the Giant's Causeway. Surfing-sized breakers curl and crash onto the beach. It is a dogleg left to a plateau green above a bend in the river. The fairway slopes left towards the river and is classic links land – one bad bounce and you're in the Bush. The 2nd/11th (par 3) has an undulating green with the river at the back. (The 11th is played from a different, elevated, tee box.) At the 4th tee, the river turns away from the dunes and flows along ploughed fields. The next three holes are played over parkland. The 4th and 5th are along the river. Don't hook your drive – especially at the 5th where there is a weir to the left of the tee. The Giant's Causeway and Bushmills Railway crosses the 7th par 3. It's built on part of a tramway which once carried visitors from Portrush to the Causeway. "In Summer, the electric tram stops and lifts passengers every hour at the Clubhouse" said the Irish Golfing Guide published in 1910. The tramway – the first hydro-electric tram in Europe, was in use from1883 until 1949. Across the track you are back on links land for the finishing three holes. The 9th/18th is all bumps and hollows back to the clubhouse. Don't be misled by the charm of Bushfoot and the reminder of more leisurely times when a golfer could travel to the course by tram. It is no pushover.

THE VALLEY COURSE – ROYAL PORTRUSH
18 holes – par 70 (5645metres/6273yards)
On the edge of Portrush on the coast road from Bushmills.
Green Fees: £25 weekdays, £32 weekends and bank holidays.
Telephone: 028 70 822311

Like Royal County Down, Royal Portrush has three clubs and two courses. The Royal Portrush men's club, the Royal Portrush ladies' club and the affiliated "townsmen's" Rathmore Club; the championship "Dunluce" course and the Valley course. Visitors to the Valley course pay their green fees at the smart new Royal Portrush clubhouse and walk back down the 18th to the Valley course beside the ladies' clubhouse. The Valley was built as a separate ladies' course in 1894. The ladies were soon to win all the honours for the club. May Hezlet – whose portrait hangs in the ladies' clubhouse – won the Ladies' British Open Amateur Championship in 1899 (a week after her seventeenth birthday) and again in 1902 and 1907. Her sisters, Florence and Violet, were finalists on three other occasions. Were it not, literally, overlooked by the great "Dunluce" links, the Valley would be much better known. It lies in a hollow between the sand-hills at the back of the East Strand and the higher ground of the more exposed championship course. The design was dictated by naturally occurring features. The fairways are generous, the hazards are the bumps, hollows and ridges of the classic links. The greens are less straightforward than they seem and the course is very lightly bunkered. There are no bunkers on the opening hole, but the 2nd green is defended by four bunkers – a fifth of the total number on the course. Wild roses line the path to the 3rd tee for the first of five excellent par 3s. The 4th (par 5) takes you over a ridge of dunes and into the natural basin, below sea level, which contains much of the links. You can hear, but not see, the Atlantic breaking on the East Strand on the other side of the sand-hills. To the right of the 4th fairway is the chasm across which the famous "Calamity" par 3 on the Dunluce links is played. (You can see the "Calamity" tee-box high above the Valley 4th green.) The 7th fairway narrows dramatically 119metres/130yards from the green. The 8th (par 4) is a difficult dogleg right. The 9th is a dogleg left to a green hidden behind a ridge. The back nine begins with the aptly named "Switch Back" which twists right and then left over a series of steep ridges. The 12th requires a well-placed tee-shot to the narrowing fairway. The 16th with out-of-bounds all down the right, has a perfectly placed bunker on the left. A well-bunkered par 3 provides a strong finish. The course is maintained in the traditional links manner by Royal Portrush head greenkeeper, Joe Findlay, and his team. There is no spraying in the rough where larks nest and orchids and wild roses bloom. Sand martins nest in the dunes along the left-hand side of the 17th fairway. Like the larks, they nest in peace.

Strand Golf Course, Portstewart

PORTSTEWART

"Strand Course" 18 holes – par 72 (6784metres/7537yards)
West of the town, beside the entrance to the strand.
Green Fees: £50 weekdays, £70 weekends and bank holidays.
Telephone: 028 70 832015

The Northern Constitution leader-writer was in lyrical mood in the summer of 1933 as he contemplated the pleasant seaside town of Portstewart. "Men pretend that they go for golf, and better golfing they will not find anywhere, but in the depths of their hearts they go to the wind blown spaces in search of beauty and to hear the old music that has been played there for a million years – the lark's song, the sound of the waves, the curlew's call, the plover's flute – and inhale an air that is at once redolent of the mountains and the sea, the fragrance of flowers and the faint piquant incense of a thousand turf fires in the mountain homes across the Bann." The Strand links has changed since then, but only to encompass more wind blown spaces and bring the golfer closer to the sound of the sea. The 1st is often described as the best opening hole in golf. The tee is high above the fairway. To your right, Atlantic waves break on Portstewart strand. To your left, the links rolls away towards the River Bann. The fairway seems very far below. It's a dogleg right. The green is tucked into the towering sand-hills at the back of the strand. The 2nd takes you up into the dunes to another elevated tee from which you drive through a gap to a narrow upward-sloping fairway and green. It's an exhilarating start to a course that is never dull as it winds through the sand-hills and along the mouth of the Bann. The 4th "Thistly Hollow"(par 5) begins a wonderful sequence of holes in the dunes including the "Five Penny Piece" where you pitch into a green which falls off steeply all around. The 9th is a terrific par 4 – a slight dogleg left, uphill, with a big hollow on the right. The 15th is all carry to a green defended by 5 bunkers at the front. There is a slight sensation of finishing twice because the 16th and 18th both end at the clubhouse. If it's a blustery, wet day you might be tempted to cut and run. Don't. The 17th is a long par 4 demanding a precise shot to the green which falls away on all sides. Then it's back up to the clubhouse for the real finish to an unforgettable course. The club has two other courses. The 9-hole "Riverside Course" – par 64 (5324metres/5916yards) as its name suggests, runs along the River Bann on the site of the old back nine of the Strand course. The "Old Course" 18 holes – par 64 (4730metres/5256yards) is at the opposite end of the town on the site of the original club founded in 1894. In 1908 the club transferred to its present site by the strand.

CASTLEROCK
18 holes – par 73 (6499metres/7221yards)
9 holes – par 67 (4441metres/4860yards)
Entrance in Castlerock off the A2, 6 miles from Coleraine.
Green Fees: Main Course £30 weekdays (£15 for ladies), £40 weekends; Bann Course £12 weekdays, £15 weekends (day ticket).
Telephone: 028 70 848314

Castlerock owes its present layout to the great English course designer Harry Colt who revised the links in 1925, and the great Irish designer Eddie Hackett who revised it again in the 1960s. It is a cracking links. Fearsome when the wind blows hard, tough when it's calm. The greens are slick, subtly contoured and hard to read. The course is long and is crossed by a stream which comes into play on five holes. There are five par 5s (seven for ladies). It runs between the mouth of the River Bann and the Derry to Belfast railway line. The first nine holes take you right around the perimeter of the links with two of the most memorable running beside the track. You set out with the sea and the dunes on your left. The fairway dips down then up to the green. The 2nd doglegs right to take you down to the holes along the railway. The trickiest of these is "Leg O'Mutton" – a par 3 demanding absolute precision to avoid both the stream and the railway. The stream is more dangerously in play in front of the green on the 6th (par 4) which begins a series of wonderful holes. The well-bunkered 7th is played uphill to a green hidden in the dunes. The 8th doglegs right further up into the dunes. The 9th is a long par 3 with rocks and water to your left, an old quarry to your right. In the middle of the links, between the 12th green and the 13th tee is a wooden shelter shaped like a pagoda. You can check the direction of the wind on the weathervane, but it's probably from the west – which means you must play the blind tee-shot at the 15th (par 5) over a hill into the wind. From the high tees at the 16th and 17th you can see to the east the long strand at Portstewart and the north Antrim coast as far as Knocklayde, the mountain above Ballycastle. To the west are the mountains of the Inishowen Peninsula in County Donegal. You finish in grand style with two memorable par 4s from elevated tees. On the 17th watch out for the big bunker guarding the raised green. From the 18th tee you see an enormous sand-hill on your right. You cannot see the green. It is on a raised plateau behind the mound. Good luck.

The 9-hole Bann course lies between the main course and the sea. You can see it from the 18th tee on the big course. There are different tee positions out and back. The front nine is par 34, the back nine is par 33. There is one par 5 on the front nine. It's a short course, but with an even more pronounced links character than the big course. It's played through the dunes along narrow fairways to small greens and demands accurate iron play. Single figure handicappers use it to hone their game. For the rest of us, it's another charmer well worth a visit.

BEYOND THE 18TH GREEN

The architect Sir Charles Lanyon and a Scottish engineer called William Bald created the Antrim coast road in 1834 by blasting through the chalky cliffs that line the coast from Larne (Latharna – "Descendants of Lathar") to Cushendall (Bun Abhann Dalla – "Foot of the River Dall"). The road was later extended further along the coast to Ballycastle. It ended centuries of isolation for the small farming and fishing communities of the nine Glens of Antrim – Glenarm (Gleann Arma – "Glen of the Army") Glencloy (Gleann Cloiche – "Glen of the Stone") Glenariff (Gleann Airimh – "Arable Glen") Glenballyemon (Gleann Bhaile Éamainn – "Edward's Homestead") Glenaan (Gleann Athain – "Glen of the Burial Chamber") Glencorp (Gleann Corp – "Glen of Bodies") Glendun (Gleann Doinne – "Glen of the River Dun") Glenshesk (Gleann Seisc – "Barren Glen") and Glentaisie (Gleann Taise – "Taisie's Glen").

Glenariff, with its wooded slopes and waterfalls, is generally considered the most beautiful of the Glens. The bay at **Waterfoot**, where the Glenariff River flows into the sea, is 1.5km/1mile wide. At the top of the glen you can follow marked trails through **Glenariff Forest Park**. (Open daily from 10am–sunset.)

In **Cushendall**, four streets meet at the Curfew Tower – built by the local landlord Francis Turnley in 1809 as a "place of confinement for idlers and rioters." The Dall River meanders along Shore Road, through the golf course, and enters the sea under a pretty wooden bridge at the pebbled beach. At the north end of the beach, just by the entrance to the golf course, a path leads to the thirteenth-century ruins of **Layde Church** (Leithead – "Slope") in a quiet spot overlooking the sea. It was a parish church until 1790 and the burial place of the MacDonnells of Antrim. A cross marks the grave of Dr James MacDonnell, one of the organisers of the famous Festival of Irish Harpers held in 1792, and founder of the Belfast Medical School. Another stone laments the death of an 18-year-old emigrant killed in the American Civil War.

On the A2 to **Cushendun** (Bun Abhann Doinne – "Foot of the River Dun") the distinctively rounded hill is **Tiveragh** – a small extinct volcano. The neck-shaped point on **Tievebulliagh** on the left, is also evidence of the volcanic activity that shaped much of the north Antrim landscape. Porcellanite was quarried on the slopes of **Tievebulliagh** in Neolithic times. Axes, spears, hammers and scrapers from here have been found in other parts of the British Isles – evidence of a Stone Age weapons factory. Turn left into **Glenaan** and left again to **Ossian's Grave** (signposted). In legend, Ossian is the son of Finn MacCool. In reality, the grave is a megalithic court grave. There is a memorial cairn to the poet John Hewitt (1907–1987) nearby.

A detour from the A2 into **Glendun** takes you to the imposing stone viaduct with three arches built by Sir Charles Lanyon in 1839 to carry the extension of the coast road across the glen and over the Glendun River. The road back down the glen to **Cushendun** passes Craigagh Wood (Creig – "Rock"), an ancient oak wood which in the seventeenth and eighteenth centuries concealed a **Mass Rock**. The rock is carved with a crucifixion scene and is said to have been brought to the Glens from Iona. In the graveyard of Saint Patrick's Church at Craigagh, at the back of the church, is a touching headstone carved by a young girl grieving for her lover who was lost at sea. The inscription, under a ship and anchor, says: "Your ship love is moored head and starn (sic) for a fulldiew." (A "full due" was the payment given to a sailor at the end of a voyage.)

Cushendun is one of the most picturesque and least typical villages in the Glens because of the "Cornish" cottages which Lord Cushendun and his Cornish wife, Maud, commissioned from Clough Williams-Ellis. At the end of the waterfront, a cave offers the only access to a Georgian house in a small, cliff-surrounded cove.

There are two scenic roads from **Cushendun** to **Ballycastle**. The first – Lanyon's extension of the Antrim coast road – takes you over the **Glendun Viaduct** and across the Antrim Plateau. There are splendid views back over **Cushendall Bay**. On a clear day you can see the Mull of Kintyre and the islands of Sanda and Ailsa Craig – known as "Paddy's Milestone". (Sanda looks like an overturned spoon.) The second – a steep narrow road, lined with fuchsia and honeysuckle – hugs the coastline and passes **Torr Head, Murlough Bay** and **Fair Head**. There are wonderful views of the sea, Rathlin Island and the Scottish coast.

At **Torr Head** (Tor – "Rocky Height") a modern Celtic cross commemorates Shane "the Proud" O'Neill who was killed by Sorley Boy MacDonnell in 1567. Beautiful, wooded and unspoiled **Murlough Bay** (Murlach – "Sea Inlet") has a memorial to Sir Roger Casement – Republican hero to the Irish, hanged as a traitor by Britain for his part in the 1916 Rising. The bay is also associated with the legend of the Children of Lir.

The cliffs at **Fair Head** (signposted) plunge 193metres/636ft to the sea. Saint Colmcille, on his way to Iona, is said to have narrowly escaped drowning in Slough-na-Morra ("The Swallow of the Sea") – a whirlpool at the southern tip of **Rathlin Island** 5km/3miles away. **Grey Man's Path** to the bottom of the cliffs should only be attempted by those as sure-footed as the wild goats which graze the cliff-tops. On the headland are three small loughs. In the middle of the largest of them, **Lough-Na-Cranagh**, is an oval-shaped crannóg (a fortified lake dwelling) with a dry-stone revet about 6 feet above the water.

The town of **Ballycastle** (Baile Chaisleáin – "Townland of the Castle") runs uphill from the beach and harbour to the Diamond – once the site of the MacDonnell castle for which the town was named. A block of Georgian buildings now stands in its stead. Holy Trinity Church (C of I) was built in 1756 in the Greek Revival style. The Ould Lammas Fair has been held in the Diamond since 1606. Nowadays it's always on the August bank holiday Monday and Tuesday.

A flat stone with a holed cross by the church door at **Bonamargy Friary** (Bun na Margaí – "Foot of the River Margy") marks the grave of Julia McQuillan, a seventeenth-century recluse known as the Black Nun. She wanted church-goers to walk over her grave as a sign of her perpetual humility. (Friary always accessible.)

There is a daily ferry service from Ballycastle harbour to **Rathlin Island** – the largest island off the Irish coast (Reachlainn – derivation uncertain). It was known to Ptolemy as "Rikini". Like Tievebulliagh near Cushendall, it had a Stone Age axe factory which exported to other parts of the British Isles. Saint Comgall's monastery on Rathlin (founded in 508) was the first place in the

distillery in the world. There are daily tours every 30 minutes from April to October beginning 9.30am (Sundays 12 noon) last tour 4pm. In winter the tours are from 10.30am–3.30pm Monday to Friday. (Telephone: 028 207 31521)

The dramatic ruins of **Dunluce Castle** (Dúnlios – "Fortress") sit precariously above the sea on a basalt outcrop separated from the mainland by a 7metre/20ft-wide gulf. Richard de Burgh built an Anglo-Norman castle on the rock in the thirteenth century. It was captured by the McQuillans who lost it to the MacDonnells in 1565. (The MacDonnells covered bog with rushes and placed their men on firm ground. The McQuillans sank into the bog.) The castle kitchens and seven cooks fell into the sea during a storm in 1639. The MacDonnells moved to Glenarm and the castle fell into decay. The extensive ruins are a fine example of Anglo-Norman architecture. There were five circular towers joined by a curtain wall. Two of the original towers, and fragments of another two remain. A platform on the inside of the wall allowed archers to fire arrows through slits in the battlements. A drawbridge connecting the castle to the mainland could be raised against attack. Defenders could come and go through a large sea cave. Because of its impregnable position, the castle did not have a keep. A gatehouse was built around 1600.

Just past Dunluce Castle there is a panoramic view of **Portrush** (Port Rois – "Harbour of the Headland") the East Strand, the limestone cliffs known as the **White Rocks**, and the Dunluce and Valley links of **Royal Portrush Golf Club** behind the giant sand-hills of the Strand. The small islands offshore are **The Skerries** (Na Sceirí – "The Reefs"). The **White Rocks** have been weathered into columns, caves and arches. The 25metre/80ft deep **Cathedral Cave** can be explored via a steep path from the road.

Portstewart has a 5km/3mile strand which runs from the west end of the town all the way to the mouth of the River Bann. On the other side of the Bann mouth on the A2 are **Castlerock** and **Downhill**.

The A2 crosses the River Bann at **Coleraine**. On the east bank of the river, a mile south of **Coleraine** is a signpost for **Mountsandel Fort** (Dún dá Bheann – "Fort of the Two Peaks") in a commanding position on a promontory overlooking the river. Legend links this large oval-shaped mound, 61metres/200ft high, with Niall of the Nine Hostages. Archaeologists think it may be the earliest inhabited site in Ireland. Post holes from a wooden dwelling found at the site are 9,000 years old.

Downhill Palace stands on a cliff-top a mile east of **Castlerock**. The **Bishop's Gate** – a classical arch with a Gothic gate lodge – was built in 1784 by Frederick Augustus Hervey, Earl of Bristol and Bishop of Derry (1730–1803) as the main

entrance to his Irish estate. The woodland garden at the entrance was reclaimed from dereliction by a National Trust warden (Miss Jan Eccles). The path uphill through the garden leads up to the headland and the ruined palace. It is surrounded by a ha-ha – a ditch with a wall on its inner side below ground level which allowed an unimpeded pastoral view from the windows. (If you explore the roofless house you will notice the bishop's study had the best views.) The house was designed to slope from front to back towards the sea. As you walk through the ruins you see, perfectly framed in the gateway of the courtyard, **Mussenden Temple**, a classical rotunda perched on the edge of the cliff. It is exactly in line with the central axis of the house. A Latin inscription from Lucretius on the frieze around the dome translates: "It's pleasing to watch from land the great struggling of others when winds whip up the waves on a mighty sea." Directly below, the railway line from Belfast to Derry cuts through the cliff. On the left, you can see miles of pale gold strand and the hills of Donegal. Castlerock, the Bann mouth and Portstewart Strand are to the right. From inside the rotunda the temple seems to be floating high above the sea with aerial views of the coast and the sea birds below. Extraordinary. (Grounds always open. Temple open weekends Easter to October, noon–6pm. Open daily July and August. Telephone: 028 70 848728)

TOURIST INFORMATION

Ballycastle Tourist Information Centre: Sheskburn House,
7 Mary Street, Ballycastle
Telephone: 028 207 62024
Giant's Causeway Tourist Information Centre:
Tel: 028 207 31855
Portrush Tourist Information Centre: Dunluce Castle,
Sandhill Drive, Portrush BT56 8BF
Telephone: 028 70 823333
Coleraine Tourist Information Centre: Railway Road,
Coleraine BT52 1PE
Telephone: 028 70 344723

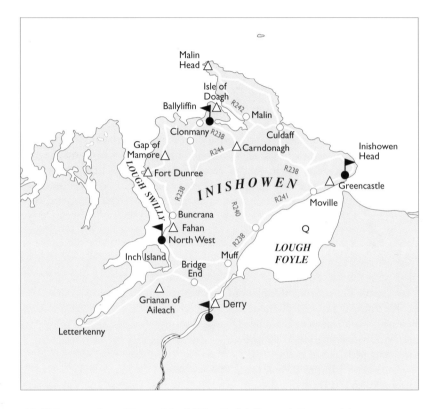

(Golf Courses: City of Derry, North West, Ballyliffen and Greencastle)

Distances: Derry to Ballyliffen 51km/32miles; Derry to Letterkenny 35km/22miles; Buncrana to Carndonagh 20km/13.5 miles.

"Very few districts have such a record of good order as Moville,
but it is characteristic of Inishowen, which is the most peaceful
place in Ireland, perhaps in the world."
(Mr Justice Walsh reported in the *Londonderry Sentinel*
22nd August 1935.)

Donegal people will tell you "a day out of Donegal is a day wasted". Why leave a county that has everything? The coastal scenery is by turns dramatic and tranquil. Waves crash against some of the highest cliffs in Europe, small stone-walled fields sweep gently to the shore, cattle graze along quiet inlets, golden beaches line the shore - all within the space of a few miles. There are 20 golf courses in County Donegal. The best of them are links courses. They include both the oldest and the newest links in Ireland. Derry City lies at the southern end of the Inishowen Peninsula and so has been included with Donegal, its natural hinterland.

Inishowen, the largest peninsula in County Donegal, reaches out into the Atlantic between Lough Foyle and Lough Swilly. At its tip is Malin Head, the most northerly point in Ireland. Inishowen (Inis Eoghain – "Eoin's Peninsula") takes its name from Eoin, one of the many sons of Niall of the Nine Hostages who ruled Ireland from Tara in the fourth century. (Another son, Conall, is commemorated in Tír Chonaill – "Land of Conall" – the Irish for Donegal.) A cluster of mountains slope to a coastline of storm beaches, rocky bays and shining golden strands. Here is some of the least known, most beautiful and varied scenery in Ireland. Most of it is a European Special Area of Conservation. The "Inishowen 100" is a signposted route of about 160km/100miles around the coastline starting and ending in the village of Bridgend 5km/4miles from Derry (Doire Cholm Cille – "Columcille's Oak Wood").

CITY OF DERRY
Prehen Course 18 holes – par 71 (5877metres/6429yards)
3 miles south of Derry off the A5 to Strabane.
Green Fees: £20 midweek; £25 weekends and bank holidays.
Dunhugh Course 9 holes – par 66 (4301metres/4708yards)
Green Fees: Daily rate £6 adults, £3 children.
Telephone: 028 71 346369

It's only three miles from the city, but the outlook from the magnificent clubhouse is completely rural. The course lies on the eastern side of the River Foyle, on a hillside that falls straight down to the main road and the shore. You look across the river to pastures and woodland dotted with farms. The already wide river widens even more upstream. The Prehen course was shaped by two masters of golf course design – Willie Park (Sunningdale) who laid out the first 9 holes in 1911, and Harry Colt (Sunningdale, Wentworth, Royal Portrush) who extended the course in 1930. It was skilfully planted with, now mature, trees positioned to please the eye and entrap the golfer. Here a clump of silver birch and beech, there horse chestnut, whitebeam and holly. At the 9th a glorious cherry abuts the fairway. (Try looking for your ball amidst the fallen blossom.) Small rows of conifers stand smartly to attention. A bank of azaleas, all reds, purples and pinks behind the 7th green, make you realise how much man has imposed on this landscape, for elsewhere glorious whins erupt from the hillside and must be kept in check. Despite its location and the many uphill and downhill lies, the course isn't too steep. From the 3rd you climb gently across the hillside to the 6th – helped by the prevailing wind – then zigzag to the 8th at the top of the course. The view changes all the time – a broadening expanse of hills upstream in one direction, and glimpses through the trees of the outskirts of the city in the other. The course feels very natural. Several holes are crossed by streams that run through dells. These make for tricky approaches to the greens, since they are sometimes invisible. (Visiting clubs say it's nearly impossible to beat the members on their own course.) There's another invisible hazard on the 2nd (par 4) where only hawthorns are in play, and the only clue to the chasm in front of the green is the hole's name – "The Valley". You won't see it from 164metres/180yards out. This is not an easy course. Decide on match play and don't mind your score if you're visiting for the first time. The clubhouse has a grandstand view of the 18th which demands a drive over a quarry. The fairway slopes left. The green is on a plateau.

The 9-hole **Dunhugh Course** lies below the **Prehen** and is less affected by the slope. It's easier and shorter, but still has some of the same character as its larger neighbour. The longest hole is 356metres/390yards (par 4) and there are five other par 4s. The green fee is the best value in Ireland. For £6 (adult) and £3 (child) you can play all day.

NORTH WEST
18 holes – par 70 (5371metres/5968yards)
1km from Fahan on the road to Buncrana.
Green Fees: IR£15 weekdays, IR£20 weekends and bank holidays.
Telephone: 077 61027

North West was founded in 1891 and in November that year, helped found the Golfing Union of Ireland. The links runs between the coast road along Lough Swilly and the water's edge. Therein lies its problem. The sea has been steadily encroaching. "The tees used to be out in sand dunes", recalls Plunkett Duffy, the head greenkeeper who has been fighting a battle against erosion for all of his 40 years at the club. Four greens have been lost to the sea in that time. The club, with the help of grants from the Royal and Ancient, energetic fundraising by the members and mighty efforts by Plunkett and his staff, has reclaimed some of the lost land and built a sea-wall of boulders to prevent further loss. The only obvious sign of this ongoing battle is at the 4th hole where the fairway swerves around land presently being reclaimed. This is a flat links. But don't be fooled. It may be flat, but it's not easy. In classic links style, the course is subtly contoured and the flatness makes it harder for the visitor to spot the strategically placed bunkers. The design is an outer and inner loop between the road and the sea-wall. The 1st is a long par 4 (par 5 for ladies) along the shore with Lough Swilly, the Fanad

Peninsula and Inch Island on your right. The next four holes run out along the shore. In summer, seals swim beside the 3rd tee from which you pitch to a well-protected, wedge-shaped green. The 6th to 10th holes run back along the road. A narrow approach to the green and a grass trap known as "The Cauldron" make the 7th the toughest hole on the course. The 8th – called "The Piffler"– is a notorious card-wrecker. The green is surrounded by bunkers, the rough at the back is deadly, the road is out-of-bounds. Beware the bunkers on the 9th. The 11th begins the inner loop. A par 4 and a par 5 provide a strong finish.

BALLYLIFFEN
Old Course 18 holes – par 72 (5745metres/6384yards)
Glashedy Links 18 holes – par 71 (6391metres/7102yards)
Just past Clonmany on the R238 to Carndonagh.
Green Fees: Old Course IR£21 weekdays, IR£24 weekends and bank holidays, IR£14 winter; Glashedy IR£30 weekdays, IR£35 weekends and
bank holidays, IR£20 winter.
Telephone: 077 76119

The north-facing hill at Ballyliffen is dark and melancholy until lit by the rays of the setting sun. The light sparkles out to sea and waves crash on to Glashedy Rock beyond the shelter of the Pollan Bay. Here, at the tip of the Inishowen Peninsula near the northern-most part of Ireland, in 360 acres of dunes, lie two wonderful golf courses. They are a contrast in styles. **Glashedy** is that uniquely Irish phenomenon, the modern links course. Most links courses were laid out in the late nineteenth and early twentieth centuries by the hand of God assisted by human designers using spades and horse-drawn machinery. Course designers can now use huge earth moving equipment to cut fairways through the dunes and lay greens in previously impossible places.

Glashedy is a big modern links, designed by Pat Ruddy and Tom Craddock, routed through the high sand-hills which dominate the links land on which both courses are played. The most memorable features are two par 3s played from the enormous ridge at the edge of the sand-hills, and the deep and daunting pot bunkers guarding most of the greens. From the 1st tee, a huge expanse of dune land stretches into the distance. As you walk to the 2nd tee, the marram grass ripples in the wind like waves on the sea. It is a wonderful sight. There is a narrow entrance to the fairway on this difficult par 4 which zigzags up to a dune-encircled green guarded by an awesome pot bunker. An equally fearsome bunker guards the 3rd green. At the 4th green you are on the top of the ridge. From the 5th tee you can see the waves breaking on the island rock that gives the course its name. (Don't miss the green on this par 3. The revetted bunkers are so deep there are steps down into them.) The 7th is an unforgettable par 3 played from the summit of the ridge down to a tiny green which seems very far below. There is a big pond to the right and pot bunkers to the left. Club selection is all. The 10th to 13th are played on the flatter ground beside the Old course. The dune-lined 12th and 13th take you back up onto the ridge. Waves pound the shore on your left. You can see in the distance the ruins of the O'Doherty castle on the Isle of Doagh. The 13th demands a long carry over waves of marram grass to the ever-narrowing fairway. The 14th is a par 3 back-to-back with the 7th – the pond below the ridge is on your left this time. Then you are routed along flatter ground towards and along the shore and the Old course, back to the clubhouse. The 17th is a long par 5 (501metres/549yards). The 18th winds through the dunes to a grandstand finish in front of the large windows of the clubhouse. Watch out for the steep revetted bunkers guarding the green. You may have an audience.

When Nick Faldo first saw the **Old Course** he thought it "the most natural course ever". He subsequently tried to buy Ballyliffen, but the members, after much discussion and debate, decided not to sell. It's easy to see what enraptured Faldo. This is golf stripped back to the very essence of the game that began on sandy, unproductive grazing ground among the dunes on the east coast of Scotland more than 500 years ago. The Old course is played over apparently flat, but always uneven, ground between the high ridge of sand-hills and the sea shore. The lies are tight, but your stance is rarely straightforward. There is usually a bump or undulation to be weighed in the balance. The 2nd bumps and undulates uphill to the green. The members say it's the toughest hole on the course. From here you can see Malin Head to the east, Dunaff Head (shaped like a sleeping rhinoceros) to the west, and Glashedy Rock out to sea. A sea of dunes surrounds you. The 5th hole, "The Tank", is an uphill par 3 into the dunes. The plateau green falls away toward bunkers. The second nine is closer to the sea. The sea roars to your left as you strike towards the tiny green on the 10th. The 13th and 14th are played from elevated tees with views out over the bay. You come closest to the waves pounding the shore on the 16th. The round finishes with a par 3 followed by a par 5 back to the clubhouse.

GREENCASTLE

18 holes – par 69 (5211metres/5703yards)
1km north of Greencastle on the east side of the Inishowen Peninsula.
Green Fees: IR£15 weekdays, IR£20 weekends and bank holidays.
Telephone: 077 81013

> *"The links at Greencastle, always in fine order, were played*
> *over constantly and visitors to the place had a fine time of it."*
> (*Londonderry Sentinel*, December 29th 1903)

Visitors to Greencastle still have a fine time. You will finish your round with a spring in your step. The design takes full advantage of the seaside setting. The 12th (par 4) is played directly over a sandy beach (in play) towards the lighthouse. (That remains your target, since you won't see the flag once you leave the high tee.) The 6th (par 4) is a sharp dogleg left to a promontory green. You'll be tempted to go straight for the green (about 183metres/200yards) but if you miss you'll be out-of-bounds on the shore. The tee boxes for several holes stand above a beach or cove. Play from the green tees to make sure you don't miss the enchanting inlet by the 5th. And the delights aren't only at the seashore. The 1st (par 4) is played round a large, rocky outcrop and across a ditch. You'll need an excellent drive to get a view of the approach to the green, let alone the flag. The 2nd (par 4) is the first of the new holes, laid out in 1991 by Eddie Hackett. These complement the old for the rising land has a springy feel, and the original nine are as much meadow as links. At the 4th tee, cattle and sheep graze the hillside above you. The skyline is dotted with the little low houses of Donegal. But your eyes will be drawn across the mouth of the Foyle to a long ridge whose great grey head is known as Campbell's Rock. The course is too exposed to have many trees, but whins and hawthorn abound. The birdsong is insistent. The 10th (par 5) sweeps you back to the shore holes and to a layout unchanged since the nineteenth century. As you turn inland at the 13th (par 5) the only clue to your direction is four little green mounds (bunkers) which give the only definition to this long dogleg across flat ground. The 14th is equally perplexing although a straight line through the ladies' tee (125metres/137yards ahead) gives the general line. The 15th (par 3) is played from a raised tee above the shore. Take a last look at the sea and the islets in the next bay. Below you, around the green is a huge patch of white and intense pink, where daisies declaim the naturalness of this lovely course. Greencastle is an active fishing port and the home of the national Fishing Training Centre and you'll see the fishing boats going about their work. (Visit the **Inishowen Maritime Memorial** outside the **Greencastle Maritime Museum** and **Planetarium** for a reminder of how dangerous their work can be. It is a simple and moving tribute to the fishermen who've lost their lives, from 1757 when the whole fleet was drowned, to the present day.)

BEYOND THE 18TH GREEN

Derry takes its name from a monastery founded by Saint Colmcille in AD546. The English first established a garrison here in 1566. In 1608 it was overrun by the O'Dohertys, the chiefs of Inishowen. In 1613, to prevent further rebellion, the city was given to the Companies of the City of London in the Plantation of Ulster. They renamed it **Londonderry** and built the walls you see today. They are over 7metres/20ft high, up to 9metres/30ft wide and 1.5km/1mile round. The city was recently renamed **Derry** by the City Council. It is the most complete walled city in Ireland – famously besieged by the troops of King James II in 1689. His failure to take the city from the defending Apprentice Boys was a decisive factor in his eventual defeat by King William of Orange at the Battle of the Boyne in 1690. You can walk around the walls, except for the section above **Saint Columb's Cathedral** (C of I). This post-Reformation cathedral was the first in the British Isles to be built by Protestants. It was founded in 1633 and restored in 1886. The London connection is spelled out on a date stone in the porch:

If stones could speake then London's prayse should sound
Who built this church and cittie from the ground.

Inside the city walls, four streets radiate from **The Diamond** to the four original gates – **Bishop Gate, Butcher Gate, Shipquay Gate** and **Ferryquay Gate**. Shipquay Street runs steeply from the Diamond to **Guildhall Square**. The **Tower Museum** at the bottom of Shipquay Street tells the history of the city. (Open daily July and August; Tuesday to Saturday, 10am–5pm rest of the year. Telephone: 028 71 372411)

From **Derry** take the A2 to **Bridgend**. Then take the N13 signposted to Letterkenny. After 1.5km/1mile turn left for **Grianán Aileach** ("The Sunny Place of Aileach") on a 244metre/800ft hill between Lough Swilly (An tSúileach – "The One with Eyes") and Lough Foyle (Loch Feabhail – possibly named for Feabhal, son of Eoin). This legendary stone-built ring-fort has been important since the second century BC. It was built around 1700BC and was known to the Alexandrian geographer, Ptolemy. The terraced walls are 5.25metres/17ft high and 4metres/13ft thick. The inner cashel is 15metres/82ft in diameter. You can see from the magnificent and commanding views over Lough Swilly and Lough Foyle why the O'Neills chose to rule most of Ulster from here. Saint Patrick is said to have baptised Eoin, son of Niall of the Nine Hostages, in the well inside the fort.

Descending from Grianan to the N13 take the R239 immediately opposite, signposted **Buncrana**. This rejoins the **Inishowen 100**. The route all the way around Inishowen is well signposted. (Don't be surprised when it takes you through a farmyard. It is very narrow in parts.) If at all possible, pick a clear day for a drive around the peninsula. The weather in Donegal is variable. Fronts roll in from the Atlantic. Some days, the sky is on the ground and visibility is very poor. But it can be fine again within a few hours. The constantly changing sky adds to the beauty of the scenery. When a trough of high pressure is established over Europe, it keeps the Atlantic fronts at bay. When that happens, Donegal is paradise.

In the Church of Ireland graveyard at **Fahan** (Fathain – "Grave") by the shores of Lough Swilly, are the vestiges of the seventh-century monastery of **Saint Mura**. In the middle of the graveyard is an upright slab with a Celtic cross carved on both sides. On the east face of the slab there are also the outlines of two birds. They may relate to the legend that birds made signs to Saint Mura to build the abbey in this lovely spot. On the west face are two figures, probably monks. The edge of the cross has the only Greek inscription known from early Christian Ireland and translates: "Glory and Honour to the Father, Son and Holy Spirit".

It indicates links between Inishowen and the wider Christian world. A second cross slab is set into the wall outside the graveyard. The crozier of Saint Mura and the shrine of Saint Mura's Bell are in the National Museum in Dublin. The bell is in the Wallace Collection in London.

Where the river flows into the sea at **Buncrana** (Bun Cranncha – "Mouth of the Crannach River") stands **O'Doherty's Keep**. The O'Dohertys were the Lords of Inishowen until Sir Cahir O'Doherty rebelled against the English and was defeated (1607). All the O'Doherty lands and castles were seized and given to the English soldier Sir Arthur Chichester. He leased it to the Vaughan family who lived in it until 1718. The keep is a mediaeval tower-house with fortifications and gun emplacements. It is in a good state of preservation. The Vaughans built **Buncrana Castle** nearby. It is noted for its panelled interior. There is a splendid seaside walk along the coast to **Ned's Point** and **Hegarty's Rock**.

North of **Buncrana** on the **Inishowen 100, Fort Dunree Military Museum** (Dún Rí – "Fort of the King") stands on a rocky promontory high above the sea. The site – signposted **"The Guns of Dunree"** – is worth a visit for the magnificent views alone. There is a small sheltered beach on your right as you approach the fort, parade ground, gun emplacements and barracks. You can see the mountains on the Fanad Peninsula across the Swilly. The Urris Hills (Iorrus – "Promontory") rise ahead. The museum, covering nearly 200 years of coastal defence history, is in the fort itself which was artificially cut off from the mainland and is accessible only across a narrow bridge. It was built in 1812 to deter invasion byNapoleon. (Museum open daily, 10am–6pm in summer. Telephone: 077 61817)

Follow the sign for the **Inishowen 100** along a river valley to the Gap of Mamore (Má Mhór – "Big Plain"). At the 262metre/860ft summit, Mamore Hill is on your right and **Dunaff Head** (Dún Damh – "Fort of the Oxen") juts out into the Atlantic before you. Enjoy one of the finest views in Donegal as you descend steeply towards Rockstown harbour and raised beach below. Lovely Leenan strand (Líonán – "Shallow Sea-bed") is on the left.

Just before **Clonmany** (Cluain Maine – "Maine's Meadow") there is a fenced track beside Glen House (private) which takes you on foot to the waterfall in **Butler's Glen**.

After **Ballyliffen** (Baile Lifín – "Liffin's Homestead") take the road signposted **Isle of Doagh** (Dumhachoileán – "Sandhill Island") – a wide peninsula lined with beautiful beaches. At the Atlantic tip of the isle are storm beaches where Atlantic waves have swept drifts of smooth, rounded rocks, pebbles and shells onto the shoreline. Here too, are the ruins of another O'Doherty castle on a rocky promontory.

The **Inishowen 100** takes you next to **Carndonagh** (Carn Domhnach – "Cairn of the Church"). Just outside the town is the oldest high cross in Ireland, dating from AD650. It marks the site of a church Saint Patrick is said to have established here in AD442. The cross is cut from a single slab of sandstone, of a type found locally and is richly carved. Two pillar stones show a bishop with a bell, book and crozier, and David carrying a sword and shield. In the nearby Church of Ireland graveyard is a cross-inscribed stone known as the **Marigold Stone** because of the design on the west face which resembles a marigold.

Malin (Malainn – "Brow") is the most northerly village in Ireland. The road from here to **Malin Head** runs along **Trawbreaga Bay** Trá Bhreige – "Treacherous Strand") to **Five Finger's Strand** (not safe for bathing). Above the strand, lovely **Lagg** Church (Lag – "Hollow") nestles under the hillside. At the entrance is the granite hexagonal baptismal font from Saint Mura's Abbey in Fahan.

The **Inishowen 100** now climbs steeply uphill to **Knockamany Bens**. There is a car park and viewpoint at **Soldier's Hill**. To your west **Dunaff Head**, **Fanad Head** and **Horn Head** reach out into the Atlantic. To the north and south below you stretch miles of golden strand. Further south, inland, you can see the highest mountain on the peninsula, **Slieve Snaght** (Sliabh Sneachta – "Snow Mountain").

At **Malin Head** turn left for **Bamba's Crown**, where there is a nineteenth-century signal tower. This is Ireland's most northerly point. There are more spectacular views over the Atlantic, the peninsulas of north Donegal and the **Garvan Isles** offshore to the north-east. You can walk along the cliff-top to a chasm called **Hell's Hole** – 76metres/250ft long, 2.5metres/8ft wide and 30metres/100ft deep – into which the tide crashes with explosive force.

Cliffs rising to 246metres/800ft line the north-east coast of the peninsula from here to **Glengad Head**. The **Inishowen 100** therefore turns south and away from the coast for a short while before regaining the coast again near **Culdaff** (Cuil Dabhcha – "Nook of Sandhills").

South-west of the village, on the inland road to **Carndonagh**, are several interesting sites. **Bocan Stone Circle**, and the nearby **Temple of Deen** (also called the Druid's Altar) are evidence of a significant Bronze Age settlement in this area. The Temple of Deen is a ruined court-cairn built around 2000BC.

The ruined **Clonca Church** (Cluain Catha – "Field of Battle") disused since 1827, was built by Protestants who were allocated land seized by Sir Arthur Chichester at the time of the Plantation of Ulster. A beautifully decorated grave slab, set into a wall, pre-dates the church. It is carved with a sword, a cross, fleur-de-lys, and a hurley stick and ball. The inscription in Scots-Gaelic translates:

> "Fergus MacAllen made this stone. Magnus MacOrriston
> of the Isles under this mound."

The remains of **Clonca Cross** stand in a neighbouring field. The shaft is 3metres/10ft tall. The arms are missing.

The **Inishowen 100** from **Culdaff** to **Greencastle** winds its narrow way inland past farmyards and across bogland until a viewpoint on the crest of a hill at **Craignamaddy** (Creig na Madaí – "Rock of the Wild Dogs"). From here you can see **Greencastle** and **Inishowen Head**, and – on the other side of **Lough Foyle** – low, sandy **Magilligan Point** (Aird Mhic Giollagáin) in County Derry. The **Inishowen 100** turns left through Stroove (An tSrúibh – "The Beak") to **Inishowen Head**. You can see the **Giant's Causeway** and **Rathlin Island** from here. The road then turns back along the shore to **Greencastle** (An Caisleán Nua – "The New Castle"). The remains of what was a new castle in 1305 when it was built by the Anglo-Norman earl, Richard de Burgh, stand east of the village. It is the only example of fourteenth-century English building in Ulster. Captured by the O'Dohertys in the fifteenth century, it passed with the rest of Inishowen to Sir Arthur Chichester at the Plantation of Ulster in 1610. The **Martello Tower** near the castle was built in 1810 to repel Napoleonic invasion.

Moville (Magh Bhile – "Plain of the Sacred Tree") was at one time a port of call for transatlantic liners and a point of departure for emigrants to the United States. Now it's a fishing port and holiday resort. The "sacred tree" refers to a site of pagan worship. It was customary to build Christian churches on pagan sites. About 2km/1.25miles north-west are the ruins of **Cooley Church** with a **High Cross** and a stone-roofed tomb (2.5metres/9ft by 2metres/7ft) known as "The Skull-House". The 3metre/10ft high cross has a round hole at the top which indicates it was made from a pre-Christian hole stone. It's thought these were for making vows. A couple about to marry would join hands through the hole, or two people would clinch a bargain. The flat stone at the base of the cross has the mark of a foot.

Ishkaheen (Uisce Caoin – "Pleasant Water") is given as the burial place of Eoin – who gave his name to the entire peninsula. According to the *Annals of the Four Masters*, in AD465 "Eoin son of Niall died…This grave is at Uisce Caoin." The **Giant's Stone** – a collapsed Bronze Age tomb – is the largest dolmen in Inishowen.

The **Inishowen 100** turns right at **Muff** to complete the circuit of the peninsula at **Bridgend**. You can follow the shores of **Lough Foyle** back to **Derry City**

Malin Head

TOURIST INFORMATION

Derry Tourist Information Centre: 44 Foyle Street,
Derry BT48 6AT
Telephone: 028 71 267284

Letterkenny Tourist Information Centre: Derry Road, Letterkenny
Telephone: 074 21160

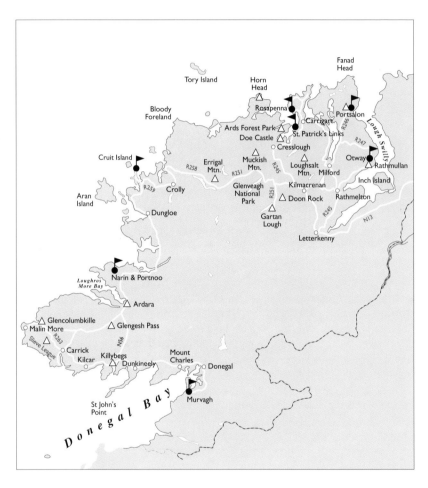

(Golf Courses: Portsalon, Otway, Rosapenna, St Patrick's Links, Cruit Island, Narin and Portnoo, and Murvagh)

Distances: Letterkenny to Donegal Town 48km/30miles; Kilmacrenan to St. Patrick's Links 24km/15miles; Kilmacrenan to Cruit Island 56km/35miles; Narin to Cruit Island 48km/30miles; Donegal Town to Killybegs 30km/18miles.

Muckish (An Mhucais – "The Pig's Back") and Errigal (An Earagail – "The Oratory") dominate the mountain ranges in north-west Donegal. Muckish looks like a turf-stack, or, as its name suggests, the back of a pig. Silvery, cone-shaped Errigal is one of the most recognisable mountains in Ireland. The Fanad Peninsula (Fánaid – "Sloping Ground") divides the open scenery of Lough Swilly from narrow and secluded Mulroy Bay, dotted with tiny wooded islands. On the western shore of Mulroy Bay (An Mhaoil Rua – "The Red Stream") are the Rosguill Peninsula (Ros Goill – "Goll's Peninsula") and the Atlantic Drive. To the southwest is Glenveagh National Park with thousands of acres of unspoiled lake and mountain scenery. In south Donegal, the wide peninsula west of **Donegal Town** pushes out in to the Atlantic between **Donegal Bay** and **Loughros More Bay** (Luacharos – "Rushy Point"). The highest sea cliffs in Europe command the tip of the peninsula at Slieve League (Sliabh Liag – "Mountain of the Pillar-stone").

PORTSALON
18 holes – par 69
On the R247 at Portsalon on the western shore of Lough Swilly.
Green Fees: IR£18 weekdays, IR£22 weekends and bank holidays.
Telephone: 074 59459

Golf has been played in Portsalon since 1891 when the club was a founder member of the Golfing Union of Ireland. In those more leisured times, long before the phenomenal growth in golf club membership, it didn't matter that fairways criss-crossed, there were a few blind drives, and the public path to the lovely beach crossed the 1st and 18th holes. The club has bought an adjoining pitch and putt course and Pat Ruddy is redesigning the layout using the additional land to lengthen fairways and take out the more hair-raising holes. The changes will make this charming course a lot safer, longer (it will be a par 72) and even more of a challenge. The setting, beside Ballymastocker Bay below the Knockalla Mountains, is magnificent. From the 1st tee – the hole is a dogleg uphill to the top of a cliff – you can admire the perfect sweep of the dune-backed bay. The sea is on your left. The 2nd is a cracking par 3 played from a tee at the rocky shoreline beneath the 1st green. Sea, beach, rocks and river-mouth are to your left, the cliff juts out to your right, the green is by a low sea-wall 180metres/197yards away. (The new layout will alter this hole. Play it before then if you can.) The 8th is another terrific par 3 with a narrow entrance to the flag-shaped green tucked into the dunes. The 13th – called "The Matterhorn" because of the pointed rock your second shot must clear – has a blind tee-shot over dunes. The 15th requires another blind tee-shot over a ridge. Your second shot must clear the river which flows in front of the green. The 17th (479metres/524yards) par 5 takes you back over the river. It's a dogleg left, with out-of-bounds on the left, and it's usually played into the prevailing wind. There's a stream to be carried on the finishing hole into the wind as well. This is classic links golf with tight lies, hard, fast greens, exhilarating views and anything from

a light breeze to a gale to test your game. You will do well to play to your handicap here. The Fanad Peninsula, while undiscovered by the rest of Ireland, is a favourite spot for people from Belfast. This makes Portsalon very busy at weekends. Try to play on weekdays when it's quieter.

OTWAY
9 holes – par 64
On the R247 3km/2miles north of Rathmullan on the western shore of
Lough Swilly. Signposted. Access through a farmyard. Pay green
fees at the farmhouse.
Green Fees: IR£10 (for the day).
Telephone: 074 58319

Otway is extraordinary. You won't have seen anything like it. Perhaps because the Fanad Peninsula is so unspoiled, this quirky relic of the Empire has been able to survive. Colonel Bill Gibson of the Irish Army (who plays at The Curragh, the oldest golf course in Ireland) in his thoroughly researched book on the origins of the game in Ireland – *Early Irish Golf* – traces the foundation of a club here to a Major Butt in 1893. He also quotes the legend that British Army officers played here in the 1850s. It is easy to imagine British Army officers, based in the martello tower on the headland at Otway, building a course to wile away the time. And what a course! The fairways are crammed into less than 35 acres of flattish links land along the shores of Lough Swilly. The 1st and 9th are between the headland and higher ground only a few hundred metres away on which are perched the 1st/10th tee and the 9th/18th green. The fairways criss-cross, the greens are surrounded by electric fencing. It's hard to tell if the sand traps are natural hazards or ancient, man-made bunkers, which have fallen in. The views across Lough Swilly are breathtaking. From the 1st tee, high above several fairways, you can see the mountains of Inishowen, Inch Island and Dunree Head. The martello tower is perched on the edge of the headland jutting into Lough Swilly. Cattle graze in fields below. The air is filled with flying balls and shouts of "Fore!" On a fine day, Otway is an enchanting place to be. On any day it will test your skill and accuracy. The 9th/18th is played from the headland across a pebble beach to the fairway. The second shot is played blind to the green high above the fairway. Unforgettable. Unmissable if you have the time. Great fun.

ROSAPENNA
Old Course 18 holes – par 70 (5723metres/6271yards)
Pat Ruddy Links 18 holes – par 71 (5986metres/6551yards)
Signposted from the R245 north of Carrigart.
Green Fees: IR£23 weekdays, IR£27 weekends and bank holidays.
Free to Rosapenna Hotel guests.
Telephone: 074 55301

Golf at Rosapenna is played in a magnificent setting on the Rosguill Peninsula between Sheephaven and Mulroy Bay. The Old course was laid out by Old Tom

Morris in 1891, and modified by some of the most illustrious designers who followed in his footsteps – James Braid, Harry Vardon, Harry Colt and CH Morrison. It was the very essence of a natural golf course. *The Sportsman's Holiday Guide 1897* said Old Tom Morris had found it necessary to lay only 3 greens – "the other 15 being natural and remarkable for their size and quality". The layout was the reverse of that we see today. The front nine began beside the original Rosapenna Hotel (destroyed by fire in 1962) and was routed over the headland between the two sea inlets. The back nine was laid out along the dunes behind the big strand – Trá Mór – along Sheephaven Bay. When the new Rosapenna Hotel was built on the other side of the road to Downings village, the order of play was reversed. Admire the splendour of the setting from the 1st green before embarking on a terrific journey along the links land at the back of the big strand. These next nine holes run between a ridge of dunes immediately behind the strand and a mountainous range of sand-hills further inland. The sea buckthorn that blooms on the ridge to your right along the 2nd and 3rd fairways was planted to combat erosion. The 3rd green is guarded by natural mounds of marram grass that will swallow your ball should you miss your target. Fairway bunkers need negotiating on the 4th. The 6th is played across the perimeter of the links before you turn back along the towering dunes in which the new holes have been constructed. You emerge from the dunes to drive across the road at the 11th and set off on a long slog up the headland. The Old course is not easy. But you are rewarded with wonderful views. From the 12th green at the summit of the hill you can look back down and see the new holes winding through the sand-hills. On the 13th – a dogleg right down to the farthest corner of the course – you look out over Mulroy Bay. Then it's uphill again to the 16th for views of the hotel between the big strand and the little strand (Trá Beag) at Downings (Na Dúnaibh – "The Forts") and Muckish Mountain across Sheephaven Bay, before launching into a glorious downhill finish.

The new links is made up of the first ten holes of the old course and eight new holes in the dunes. Eddie Hackett began work on these holes before he died but their shape today is largely the work of Pat Ruddy. The 11th cuts through the dunes to a small green in front of a huge sand-hill. The 12th is a long par 4 with an enormous crater near the narrow entrance to the green. The 13th is a magnificent par 3 over this crater. Try not to be distracted by the panoramic view of sea and mountains. You do not want to be in the crater, which is filled with water in winter. The green is your only refuge. The 15th is another par 3 over a sand crater. The 16th is a par 5 demanding a long carry to the safety of the fairway. The 18 played entirely through the dunes is already the more popular course with visitors. The Old course is traversed by the increasingly busy road to Downings. The owner and manager of the hotel and golf course, Frank Casey, intends to abandon the holes over the headland and further develop the holes in the dunes. Play the Old course before these long-term changes are complete. You will be playing a piece of golfing history.

SAINT PATRICK'S LINKS

"Magheramagorgan" 18 holes – par 72 (6438metres/7046yards)
Trá Mór 18 holes – par 71 (5320metres/5822yards)
Signposted on the R247 between Carrigart and Creeslough.
Green Fees: IR£20 weekdays, IR£25 weekends (both courses).
Telephone: 074 55114

On the road from Carrigart to Creeslough, just past the turning for Lough Salt, there's a signpost to the right for "Saint Patrick's Links". You are then directed left down a mile of rutted and pot-holed cart track to a battered caravan in the sand dunes. Beside it is a shed. Nearby, a red arrow, painted on a small white boulder, points to the 1st tee on one of the most extraordinary courses you are ever likely to encounter. "Hidden Gem" calls to mind a small course. Perhaps 9 holes in a wonderful setting, or a short, well-designed, old-fashioned 18-hole course. Saint Patrick's Links is the Koh-I-Noor and the Kimberley Diamond. There are two 18 holes links courses hidden in these dunes along Sheephaven Bay. "Magheramagorgan" is the creation of Eddie Hackett – he laid the last sod on the 16th green on 31st October 1996 – his last day's work on earth. Trá Mór is the only course in Ireland designed by a woman – Joanne O'Haire.

Magheramagorgan (Machaire Mhic Gorgáin – "Plain of the McGorgans") is named for the townland in which the links is situated. It's an appropriate name because "mahair" – the word environmentalists use to describe dune systems – is derived from the Irish word "machaire". You are certainly in the middle of a mahair here. Sand-hills tower behind you on the 1st tee. The wind blows off the sea to your right. A flag flutters at the top of the undulating, rising fairway before you. The nearest sign of other human activity is the houses beyond the coast road a mile away as you embark on the first of four par 4s. The 2nd calls for a blind tee-shot over a hill then an accurate shot through the narrow approach to the plateau green. It falls away on three sides into a pale green sea of marram grass which ripples over the dunes. The view from the green is breathtaking. Pale golden strands sweep along the bay below the unmistakeable turf-stack shape of Muckish Mountain. Black cattle graze the far edge of the links. Waves break on the big strand to your right. A huge tuft of marram grass sticks out of a natural sandbank on the left-hand side of the 3rd fairway, forcing you to play right, and not cut the corner on this dogleg to the left. The 4th is well named "Googly". You drive blind over dunes and a valley of rough to a rising fairway, which curves right and dips before rising again to a narrow entrance to the small green. If you hook your second shot you end up in a giant sand crater on the left. Draw breath at the par 3s before and after the long par 5 (468metres/512yards) 6th hole. It calls for another big carry over a valley in the dunes. At the 8th you still haven't seen a bunker. Hardly needed. It's impossible to play from a lie in the sandy dunes, which line the helter-skelter fairways. You must hit straight to avoid big trouble. The only unexciting holes are the 11th and 12th at the edge of the links where the dunes end and boggy fields begin. But big hitters will welcome the opportunity to let fly without danger of the ball being swallowed by the sand-hills. The 15th fairway ascends like a winding staircase to a green half-hidden in an amphitheatre of dunes. The spectacular view from the 16th tee, on a platform at the edge of the sand-hills, encompasses Muckish, Horn Head, Ards Forest Park on the shores of Sheephaven Bay, and the golden strands stretching towards Rosapenna and Downings. The green on this par 3 is on a platform above you. Eddie Hackett laid the last sod on this green which is why the hole is now called "Hackett's Sod". (When the greens were constructed the original turf was lifted, cut and re-laid by hand like a carpet.) The 17th is a descending staircase to a square, undulating green that rises to a peak at one corner. Then it's downhill again on a raised fairway shaped like a piece of jigsaw puzzle, falling away steeply at each side into large craters. An astonishing finish to an astonishing course.

Trá Mór ("Great Strand") is shorter, but more spectacular. From the 1st elevated tee you get a glimpse of the scenic, as well as golfing, glories ahead. With Muckish Mountain to the left you drive towards distant Horn Head, down a fairway of natural hillocks, to a green tucked into a corner behind towering dunes. The lovely, rising fairway on the 4th (par 4) runs parallel to the opening hole on Magheramagorgan with lovely views over Sheephaven Bay. Horn Head is now to your right. The 5th (par 4) rises dramatically to a naturally tiered green with a spectacular view out to sea. You are now on the edge of the dunes, with the equally dramatic 16th on Magheramagorgan to your left. Hit a good wedge from the high 6th tee. Pause to savour the magnificent panorama of Tramore strand, Ards Forest across Sheephaven Bay, Horn Head pushing out into the Atlantic and the waves crashing on the beach behind the green below. You must climb back up into the sand-hills for an exhilarating sequence of three tough holes – par 5, par 4, par 5 – before the brief respite of a relatively easy par 3 on flattish ground. There is a natural pond (complete with wild ducks) to the left of the 16th green. The 17th winds uphill through the dunes to an undulating green. The finish is magnificent. You stand on the elevated 18th tee like an eagle, surveying all around and below – the humps and bumps of the fairway stretching to the large, undulating green. The Derryveagh Mountains, Muckish, Sheephaven, and the towering sand-hills. (A golden eagle was spotted here a few years ago.) Is there a more beautiful site for a golf links anywhere on earth?

CRUIT ISLAND
9 holes – par 68 (4860metres/5400yards)
2 km/1.25miles from Kincasslagh on R257.
Green Fees: IR£10 weekdays, IR£12 weekends and July/August.
Telephone: 075 43296

On the beautiful coast road near Kincasslagh (Cionn Caslach – "Head of the Sea-inlet") a modest sign points down a narrow road to the sea and unexpectedly bears the legend "Galfchúrsa". Follow the road down to the shore, bear right past the cemetery, along the shoreline, and cross the causeway to Cruit Island, past the fishing boats lolling on the beach waiting for the incoming tide and the thatched cottages puffing peat-scented smoke into the air, to find a heavenly 9-hole links. The stiff Atlantic breeze ensures no hole plays the same way the second time around. Just to be sure, there's a second set of tees to play off. Steady your nerves as you tee up on the 6th – a par 3 played across a rocky inlet to a small green which falls steeply to the ocean behind. You can play Cruit Island all the year round. It's busy enough in the summer when the bar in the small clubhouse is open and will take your green fees. Out of season you can have it all to yourself. The views from every part of the course are magnificent. Just put the green fee in the honesty box and enjoy golf as it used to be played when the game was first invented about 500 years ago.

NARIN AND PORTNOO
18 holes – par 69 (5284metres/5872yards)
At Narin on the R261 north of Ardara.
Green Fees: IR£17 weekdays, IR£20 weekends and bank holidays.
Telephone: 074 45107

Like all links courses, Portnoo – as it's usually called – is playable all year round. Between October and March some local rules come into play. "A ball striking fencing between player and flag of hole being played may be replayed. A ball lying close to greens fencing may be dropped back within one club length not nearer the hole without penalty. A ball may be cleaned and dropped within one club length without penalty if manure interferes with stroke or stance." Links land was originally used for grazing. At Portnoo, the land nearest the clubhouse is still used for grazing cattle in the winter months. You are likely to find a couple of cows and their calves watching you tee off at the opening hole as you flight your ball towards a green surrounded by electric fencing. The second hole is a dogleg right which curves around a lake where 25 pairs of wild swans spend the winter. The next two holes take you further along the perimeter of the course towards the sea. Then you dogleg left and up into the dunes for your first clear view of the curving strand and giant sand-hills along Gweebarra Bay. The finest views are from the elevated blue tees on the 9th. Behind you is a beach and, in the distance, the Blue Stack Mountains. Before you lies another lovely strand. The fairway is a roller coaster of ridges and hollows all the way to the green out on a promontory. The 12th is another roller coaster among the dunes. The 14th is a downhill dogleg right to a green tucked up in the dunes and guarded by beautifully revetted bunkers. Portnoo is blessed with as fine a set of par 3s as you'll find anywhere. If you play them well, you're likely to return a good score. The 8th is a terrific par 3 over a valley in the dunes to a plateau green with great views from tee and green. (Wind behind, take a wedge. Wind against, take a driver.) The 13th curves around an enormous sand-hill. The last, and shortest, of the par 3s – the 16th – is known as the High Altar because of the number of good scores sacrificed on it. The neatly revetted bunkers and surrounding small dunes will catch any less than perfect tee-shot. This is a very popular course in the summer holidays when you will need to book several days in advance. It's well worth a visit anytime of the year.

MURVAGH
18 holes – par 73 (6249metres/6943yards)
Signposted off the N15 between Laghey and Ballintra.
Green Fees: IR£25 Monday–Thursday, IR£30 weekends,
IR£40 husband and wife.
Telephone: 073 34054

Murvagh (Murbhach) means salt marsh. To golfers it means lark-song, springy turf, and a marvellous sense of space. The links, designed by Eddie Hackett, lies on a promontory in Donegal Bay, beyond Murvagh forest. There are splendid mountain and sea views all around. The course signals its honesty on the opening hole. From the 1st tee you can see straight ahead a beautiful bunker smack in the middle of the fairway just short of the slightly raised green. The 3rd, 4th and 5th take you out to the end of the promontory. A stream comes into play on the 4th (par 5 for ladies) but the real challenge on this outward nine is the aptly named "Valley of Tears" – the (par 3) 5th that takes you into the sand dunes. Your drive must land on, and hold, the narrow plateau green – ringed with dunes, and falling away into an enormous bunker at the front. The 6th begins a marvellous sequence of long holes – par 5, par 4, par 5, par 4 – through the dunes along the other side of the peninsula. From the elevated tees you can see the quiet waters of Donegal harbour meeting the rougher Atlantic waves. The 7th green is hidden in the dunes. The 8th twists and bends over hummocks and hollows to a well-defended entrance to the narrow green. Enjoy the sea views from the 9th tee. The back nine are laid out in an inner loop that is more secluded, but no less wonderful to play. The 12th (par 5) is the longest hole on the course – 543metres/594yards from the championship tees. The 14th is another long par 5 – 439metres/480yards from the ladies' tee – with a stream crossing the fairway about 100metres/110yards from the green. But don't be alarmed by the overall length of the course. There are five tee positions (including the ladies' tee). You don't have to be a huge hitter to enjoy Murvagh, but you do need to be straight. The larks seem to sing more sweetly here than on any other Irish links. (The 15th is called "The Larks".) There are wild pansies in the rough. And Murvagh never feels crowded, even when it's busy.

BEYOND THE 18TH GREEN

The N13 from **Derry** cuts across the base of the **Inishowen Peninsula** and follows Lough Swilly down to **Letterkenny**, the gateway to north and west

Donegal, at the head of the lough. Originally a small fishing village, it is now the fastest growing town in Europe. The N56 from here goes through **Kilmacrennan** from where roads lead to the **Fanad Peninsula**, the **Rosguill Peninsula**, **Mulroy Bay**, **Sheephaven**, the **Derryveagh Mountains** and **Glenveagh National Park**.

The ruined Franciscan abbey at Kilmacrennan (Cill Mhic Réanáin – "Church of the Sons of Eanan") was built by the O'Donnells in the place where Saint Colmcille said to have received his education. Doon Rock, 3km/2miles north-west (signposted off the N56) was the inauguration site of the O'Donnell chieftains. Doon Well, nearby, is popularly believed to have healing powers.

The R249 from **Kilmacrennan** goes to **Rathmelton**, a pretty Plantation town built by the English and Scots settlers who replaced the rebellious Irish landowners in the early seventeenth century. The river Leannan (An Leanainn – "The Watery One") flows into Lough Swilly here and the town's past prosperity – visible in the fine Georgian houses and the warehouses along the quay – was built on trade by sea. The first Presbyterian church in the United States was founded in Virginia in 1706 by the Reverend Francis Makemie who emigrated from here. **The Old Meeting House** where he used to preach has been restored and is used as an exhibition centre.

The scenic R247 runs north along Lough Swilly to **Rathmullan** (Rath Maolaín – "Maolan's Ring-fort"). In 1587 Red Hugh O'Donnell was enticed into boarding a ship here and was taken hostage by the English who incarcerated him in Dublin Castle for four years before he managed to escape and make his way back to Donegal in the depths of winter. This and other stories are told in the **Flight of the Earls Heritage Centre** which commemorates Hugh O'Donnell and Hugh O'Neill, the last two great Irish chieftains to be defeated in the Elizabethan conquest. They fled for France from here in 1607 and their estates were confiscated. The ruined **Carmelite Priory** was built in 1508 by Rory McSweeney. The McSweeneys were gallowglasses – Scots mercenaries who came to Ireland in the fifteenth century to fight for the O'Donnells.

The R247 continues along the western shores of Lough Swilly and around the edge of **Knockalla Mountain** to **Ballymastocker Bay** and **Portsalon**. You can drive (ten minutes) or walk (one hour) a pretty circular route on the headland by taking the lane almost immediately opposite the golf club entrance. There are lovely views of **Dunaff Head** – shaped like a sleeping rhinoceros. Through **Ballydaheen Japanese Garden** you can reach **The Seven Arches** – a natural grotto with a waterfall and arches leading through caves to the open sea. (Open May to September, Thursday and Saturday 10am–3pm.)

Take the R246 across the peninsula to **Kerrykeel**. From here to **Milford** (Baile na nGallóglach – "Town of the Gallowglasses") **Mulroy Bay** with its myriad wooded

Bluestack Mountains

islands is on your right. At **Milford** take the R245 which hugs the bay most of the way to **Carrigart** (Carraig Airt – "Art's Rock") at the neck of the **Rosguill Peninsula**.

Turn right just outside **Carrigart** for **Rosapenna**, **Downings** and **The Atlantic Drive** which circles the head of the **Rosguill Peninsula**. It is just 12km/7.5miles

long and is worth walking or cycling if you have the time. The views are superb. **Horn Head** (Corrán Binne – "Crescent of the Cliff") juts out into the Atlantic on the other side of **Sheephaven Bay** (Cuan na gCaorach – "Bay of the Sheep"). To the south you can see **Muckish** and **Errigal** mountains. **Tranarossan Strand** sweeps up to **Melmore Head** at the tip of the peninsula. The road winds back above quiet **Mulroy Bay** to **Downings** and **Rosapenna**.

Return to the R245. Just before **Creeslough** (An Craoslach – "The Gullet") the romantic ruin of fortified **Doe Castle** stands on a low rocky promontory defended on three sides by the sea, and by an artificial ditch on the landward side. Cross the stone bridge over the Lackagh River and follow the signs to the castle. The powerful, square 17metre/55ft-high keep is surrounded by a bawn and a high curtain wall with round towers. It was the stronghold of the McSweeneys in the late sixteenth and early seventeenth centuries. The McSweeney chieftains are buried in the adjoining graveyard.

Ards Forest Park across an inlet in the bay, is the most northerly forest park in Ireland. The trees grow right to the water's edge, but there are also beaches where you can swim. **Lough Lilly**, which is covered with flowering waterlilies in summer, lies at the eastern edge of the forest.

You can get to **Cruit Island** and the lovely coastal scenery of **The Rosses** (Na Rosa – "The Promontories") either by continuing on the very scenic coast road past **Horn Head** and **Bloody Foreland** (Cnoc Fola – "Hill of Blood") – or by taking the R251 past **Errigal Mountain** to join the coast road. The drive to the top of **Horn Head** is a stunning 20-minute detour. Take the first turn left after the signpost for the headland and drive the circular route in a clockwise direction. Then you can really enjoy the view on the descent. **The Rosses** and **Gweedore** (Gaoth Dobhar – "Estuary of the Dobhar") are in the centre of the biggest Gaeltacht – Irish-speaking area – in Donegal. (County Donegal has the largest number of native Irish speakers in Ireland.)

You can also take a number of routes to **Glenveagh National Park** (signposted from the N56). One of the most scenic is the road which skirts **Lough Salt** (signposted just outside **Carrigart** on the R245). It climbs steeply from the coast and there is a fine view back over **Sheephaven** and **Glen Lough** from the crest of the hill before the road dips and bends to take you along the shores of **Lough Salt** within inches of the water. The road takes you back to the N56 at **Kilmacrennan**. **Errigal** and the **Derryveagh Mountains** (Sléibhte Dhoire Bheitheach – "Mountains of the Oak-Grove of the Birches") dominate **Glenveagh National Park** (Gleann Bheatha – "Glen of Birch"). At the centre of the park, in a deep, gorge-like valley, lies long, narrow **Lough Veagh** (Loch Beathach – "Birch Lough"). Mountains rise precipitously from its shores. Waterfalls tumble down the rocky slopes of **Dooish Mountain** (Dubhais – "Black Ridge") into the south-west corner of the lough. On the eastern shore of the lough stands **Glenveagh Castle** – built as a hunting lodge in the Victorian Gothic style by the local landlord, George Adair. It was presented to the Irish nation in 1983 by Henry McIlhenny, the American Tabasco Sauce millionaire whose grandparents came from Donegal. He bought the castle in 1937 and restored its gardens to their present glory. They are the finest gardens in Donegal and include a walled potager, an Italian statuary garden, a rhododendron walk leading to a panoramic viewpoint and an azalea-lined terrace constructed by recuperating Belgian soldiers during the First World War. Red deer roam the park. Peregrine falcons nest in the mountains. Cars are not allowed beyond the castle car park. There is a shuttle-bus or a 45-minute walk along the lough to the castle and gardens. (Castle and gardens open from Easter to October. Telephone: 074 37090)

George Adair was notorious for evicting 244 tenants in 1861 before he built **Glenveagh Castle**. The site of an eviction cottage is marked by a plaque near **Gartan Lough** (Gartán – "Small Field") on the R251 from Glenveagh.

The artist **Derek Hill** has also donated his house, **Saint Columb's**, which overlooks **Gartan Lough**, the birthplace of Saint Colmcille (also called Columb or Columba). The garden slopes to the water's edge. It was laid out with the help of James Russell, who helped design Henry McIlhenny's garden at Glenveagh. **Glebe House Gallery** – on the site of a fifteenth-century O'Donnell fort – houses Derek Hill's fine collection of paintings, ceramics and textiles, including work by Picasso, Bonnard, Kokoshka, Jack Yeats, Pasmore, Annigoni and Derek Hill himself. (Open mid-May to late September, 11am–6.30pm. Telephone: 074 37071)

The **Colmcille Heritage Centre** (signposted nearby) features an audio-visual presentation about the life and times of **Saint Colmcille** who was born in **Gartan** in AD521. He epitomised the missionary zeal of the early Irish monks. He set up monasteries in Derry, Durrow (County Offaly) and Moone (County Kildare). He left Ireland to found a mission on the Scottish island of Iona after an argument with another monk.

COLMCILLE'S FAREWELL

How quickly my coracle speeds on,
The salt spray blinds my gaze,
I grieve on the trackless sea,
Sailing from Ireland to Alba of the Ravens.

The cliffs grow small,
As though a mist of death my eyes look back,
I shall never see again,
The wives of Ireland or their men.

Donegal Town (Dún na nGall – "Fort of the Foreigners") was established by Red Hugh O'Donnell who built a castle and established a Franciscan friary here in the fifteenth century. The ruins of the castle stand on a rocky height above the Diamond (the town square). The ruined friary is south of the town where the River Eske (Iasc – "Fish") flows into the sea. Only the chancel and a gable of the south transept of the church, and the remains of the cloister survive. Three tutors to the O'Donnells who stayed at the friary wrote The Annals of the Four Masters – an early seventeenth-century history of Ireland. They are commemorated on an obelisk in the Diamond.

As you proceed west on the R263 coast road you can see across **Donegal Bay** to **Ben Bulben** (Beann Ghulbain – "Gulban's Peak") in County Sligo. To the northeast are the **Blue Stack Mountains** (An Chruach Ghorm – "The Blue Stack"). **Killybegs** (Na Cealla Beaga – "The Little Churches") is Ireland's biggest fishing port, and marks the start of some spectacular coastal scenery where the mountains are close to the sea. Leave the R263 at the signpost for **Kilcar** and cling even more closely to the coast by **Muckros Head** (Mucros – "Pig Promontory"). From here you can see the mouth of **Teelin Bay** (Teileann – "Dish") and, rising high above its western shore, the jagged outline of Slieve League.

Continue down the eastern shore of **Teelin Bay** to **Carrick** (An Charraig – "The Rock") at the head of this very tidal bay. Turn left down the western shore to the bay for the road to **Slieve League**. A walking route up the eastern flank of the mountain is clearly signposted. You can drive or walk 3km/2miles to the highest sea-cliffs in Europe by taking the road to the right at the school in **Teelin** village. It is a lovely road. The view changes at every turn and you can walk out to old lookout posts perched above the roaring sea. At the top of the cliffs the view is breathtaking. Across a small bay the multi-coloured mica cliffs fall 606metres/1990ft from the craggy summit to the sea. Below, in the curve of the cliffs, two huge rocks, named, as their shapes suggest, the Giant's Chair and Writing Table, rise above the waves. You can follow a track up along the cliffs, but the actual summit can only be reached across a narrow ledge with the sea 606metres/1990ft below on the left, and a sheer drop into a tarn on the right. Only for the sure-footed with nerves of steel.

The R263 west of **Carrick** takes you to **Glencolmcille** (Gleann Cholm Cille – "Colmcille's Glen"). This quiet valley at the head of **Glen Bay** contains many early Christian monuments, including an oratory, a holy well and Stations of the Cross. These are from a later date than Saint Colmcille, but there is a tradition that the saint had a battle here with demons who had evaded Saint Patrick and the monuments bear dedications to Saint Colmcille (Columba). Some would say the saint associated with **Glencolumcille** is Father McDyer who founded a rural co-operative here in the 1950s when emigration was killing the community. He gave new life to the area and put it on the tourist map. **The Folk Village And Museum** represents three centuries of rural life in the glen. In the graveyard of the Church of Ireland parish church there is a ninth-century stone-roofed souterrain. The road past the church goes to **Glen Head** which falls precipitously 213metres/700ft to the sea. It is best reached on foot. Only the first part of the road is safe to drive.

The road to **Ardara** (Ard an Rátha – "Height of the Fort") is through **Glengesh** (Gleann Gheise – "Glen of the Prohibition") – a high mountain pass. **Maghera Caves** are signposted on the approach to **Ardara**. The road to the caves runs along the seashore and cuts through rocky cliffs with waterfalls. You can park at a cottage and walk along a track through a farm and across sand dunes to the caves and a huge strand – surely one of the most secluded and beautiful in Ireland.

The Catholic church in **Ardara** has a stained glass window by **Evie Hone**. **Ardara Heritage Centre** (telephone: 075 41704) tells the story of Donegal tweed.

A road signposted **Rosbeg**, to the left off the R261 to **Narin**, leads to **Lough Doon**. (Turn left again past the school.) There is a 2,000-year-old circular stone fort on an island in the lough. The road past the lough will take you into **Narin** (An Fhearthainn – "The Rain") and **Portnoo** (Port Nua – "New Port"), the twin resorts on **Gweebarra Bay** (Gaoth Beara – "Estuary of the Bior"). A ruined chapel on **Inishkeel Island** (Inis Chaol – "Narrow Island") can be reached on foot when the tide is out. The chapel contains round stones which are believed to cure rheumatism.

The R261 joins the N56 west of **Narin** and takes you back to **Killybegs** and **Donegal Town**.

TOURIST INFORMATION

Donegal Town Tourist Information Centre: The Quay, Donegal Town
Telephone: 073 21148

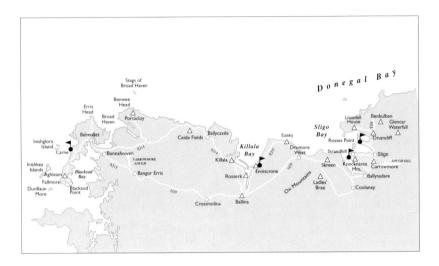

(Golf Courses: Carne, Enniscrone, Strandhill and Rosses Point)

Distances: Sligo to Enniscrone 61km/38miles; Sligo to Ballina 58km/36miles; Ballina to Belmullet (via coast) 77km/48miles; Ballina to Belmullet (inland) 61km/38miles; Belmullet to Blacksod Point 21km/13miles.

> *"...seaside golf cannot be played without thinking. There is always some little favour of wind or terrain waiting for the man who has judgement enough to use it, and there is a little feeling of triumph, a thrill that comes with the knowledge of having done a thing well when a puzzling hole has been conquered by something more than mechanical skill. And let me say again that our American courses do not require, or foster, that type of golfing skill."* (Bobby Jones)

Ireland has 40 per cent of all the links courses in the world and the west coast from Rosses Point in County Sligo to Erris Head in County Mayo has as fine a stretch of links courses as you'll find anywhere. Majestic sand dunes, fast greens, tight lies, and springy turf delight the golfer. Along this coast, archaeologists have found evidence of the earliest inhabitants of Ireland. Traces of their houses, graves and farming methods can be seen at Carrowmore near Sligo, and the Ceide Fields on the north coast of Mayo. The Mullet Peninsula is one of the last refuges of the corncrake – a bird once common in Ireland, now on the edge of extinction because of mechanised mowing. Corncrakes are shy and secretive birds, which nest in meadows. When hay was cut by hand, farmers could leave nests undisturbed. Now grants are offered to farmers who delay mowing and protect corncrake nests. The unmistakeable "crek-crek" calling of the male can be heard over long distances in spring and summer. You may hear it on the 3rd green at Carne.

CARNE
18 holes – par 72 (6119metres/6697yards)
Signposted from Belmullet, County Mayo.
Green Fees: IR£25 per day March to October, IR£38 husband and wife; IR£15 November to February, IR£25 husband and wife.
Telephone: 097 82292

Carne was built by the community of Belmullet to encourage tourism in this lovely yet largely unknown and underdeveloped part of Ireland. Visitors are guaranteed a game. Carne never turns anyone away. "If ever the Lord intended land for a golf course, this is it" said the great Irish golf architect, the late Eddie Hackett, when he first set eyes on it in 1984. This course is a passport to heaven. The setting is magnificent. From the car park in front of the clubhouse, you can see the natural harbour of Broad Haven divided from Blacksod Bay by the narrow strip of land connecting the Mullet Peninsula to the rest of north Mayo. To your right, reaching far out into the Atlantic, are Achill Island and its mountains, Slievemore and Croaghaun with its distinctive saddle shape sloping down to Achill Head. Rising on your left is the 1st hole – Cnoc na Rós ("Hill of Roses") – a dogleg, uphill over bumps and hollows to an undulating green which bends around a sand-hill. Low-growing Burnet roses bloom on the hill in summer. The 2nd is a par 3 over a valley to a green nestling in sand-hills and guarded by a neatly revetted pot bunker. The 3rd is from a tee high in the dunes to a fairway running along the north-eastern boundary of the course. (The ladies' tee – as on most of the holes – is quite far forward.) Cattle graze the fields on the other side of the fence, but the fairway has the unmistakeable spring of the true links. This is a very natural course. Not much bulldozing was needed. On the back nine holes the natural turf of bent and fescue was cut and re-laid for the greens – making them much faster than the front nine, which were seeded. On several holes – the 5th, 6th, 12th and 15th, for example – a narrow approach to the greens makes it essential to place your drive perfectly if you want to make par. The 8th – "Log 'a Si" (The Fairy Hollow) – has a blind approach to the subtly undulating, two-tiered green, snug in a hollow surrounded by dunes and protected by a deep bunker. On the 10th – "Macalla" (Echo) – you can see a

Carne Golf Course, Belmullet

curving wall of dunes, but you can't see the green, which is in a hollow. The sand-hill rises behind it in terraces, like a Greek or Roman amphitheatre. The land was previously commonage used for grazing. The terracing was created over the years by cattle trampling up and down the dunes – just another unique feature of Carne. The 11th and 12th are sharp doglegs left and right around enormous sand-hills. There are splendid views of the Atlantic Ocean, the Inishkea islands and Inishglora (where the legendary Children of Lir spent their last 300 years as swans). Bunkers and sand-hills guard the very narrow approach to the 15th green. The 17th is well named "An Muiríneach" (Marram Grass). Huge sand valleys bristling with marram grass lie to the right and left zof the ridged fairway. The wildly undulating 18th, with a deep valley and out-of-bounds on the right, makes a dramatic finish.

ENNISCRONE
18 holes – par 73 (6245metres/6835yards)
On the R297 at Enniscrone.
Green Fees: IR£20 weekdays, IR£25 weekends, December to February;
IR£26 weekdays, IR£35 weekends, March to November; IR£38 weekdays,
IR£48 weekends, husband and wife.
Telephone: 096 36297

Until 2000, Enniscrone was a highly regarded 18-hole links, which included several flattish holes between a magnificent expanse of high duneland and the

estuary of the River Moy. By cutting holes through the sand-hills, the golf designer Donald Steel has created an 18-hole links routed entirely through the towering dunes along beautiful Enniscrone strand. The club has acquired the land beside the opening holes on the previous layout. A 9-hole links is being created by adding three holes to the six existing estuary-side holes. It will open with two par 5s in succession – allowing you to open your shoulders and let fly – followed by a par 3 to remind you accuracy is as important as length. (If you are playing the 9-hole course in spring, look out for the March hares. They streak across the fairways and sport in the rough.) The new **18-Hole Links** begins near the starter's hut with a well-bunkered dogleg right up into the sand-hills. The next three holes – two par 5s and a par 3 – take you into the heart of the dune system. The 8th falls away to the right into a hollow in the dunes. The 9th needs no bunkers. It requires a huge carry over a ravine to a narrow fairway which twists from right to left. There's a big dip before the plateau green, cut into a sand-hill. There is a wonderful view of Killala Bay, Enniscrone strand, the Moy and the Ox mountains from the high 10th tee. The hole is a dogleg right to a secluded green tucked into a dell in the dunes. The 13th is a long par 3 uphill – very tough when the wind is blowing off the sea. You have a panoramic view over both courses, and the backdrop of sea and mountains, from the 14th tee. Ladies drive blind over a sand dune. Only a daunting group of pot bunkers is visible on this sharp dogleg left. The 17th is a par 3 to a small, narrow green overlooking the sea. The 18th brings you back downhill to the clubhouse.

STRANDHILL

18 holes – par 69 (5516metres/6032yards)
On the R292 west of Sligo.
Green Fees: IR£25 weekdays, IR£30 weekends and bank holidays.
Telephone: 071 68188

From everywhere on this magnificently scenic links you can see the great, towering shape of Knocknarea Mountain which dominates the landscape of the entire peninsula on which Strandhill is situated, between the mountain and the sea. If you climb to Queen Maeve's Cairn on top of Knocknarea and walk to where the mountain begins its steep descent, you will see the links laid out below you, with Sligo Bay on the right, Ballisodare Bay on the left, and in the distance the Ox Mountains in County Mayo. At Strandhill, natural splendour surrounds you – mountains, sea, towering dunes, surfing waves that pound the strand, bright red butterflies (in spring and summer) and, always, a chorus of larks. The opening hole is sedate enough. It runs along the eastern boundary of the links, below the mountain. To the right you can see the high ridge of dunes at the back of the strand. The fairway bumps and hollows will become more pronounced later in the round. The 2nd and 3rd run along Culleenamore strand on Ballisodare Bay. The 4th – a short par 4 – takes you up to a plateau green in the dunes, but beware the large bunker in the hillside in front of the green. From the 5th tee, on the highest part of the course, you can appreciate the beauty of the setting before driving to the most knobbly, bumpy and extraordinarily contoured fairway you are ever likely to see. On the 6th you first hear, then see the Atlantic breakers pounding the strand. The 7th is played alongside it. Strandhill's most famous hole is the 13th – a sharp dogleg right. You hit downhill to a plateau, then pitch to a hidden green that looks no bigger than a postage stamp. The only access is a narrow entrance between two sand-hills. The 15th climbs in stages like a staircase to the green. The 18th is a tough finish for men – a long par 4 (par 5 for ladies) dogleg right with a water hazard along the right-hand side and a difficult, uphill approach to the green. It is stroke index 1 for men (index 6 for ladies). Head greenkeeper Steve Urwin and his team emphasise the natural features of the links. They don't fight nature by trying to eradicate meadow grass from the greens, yet these run fast and true. Strandhill is a real golfing gem.

COUNTY SLIGO

"Rosses Point" 18 holes – par 71 (6041metres/6712yards)
"Bowmore" 9 holes – par 70 (5570metres/6096yards)
On the R291, signposted from Sligo.
Green Fees: "Rosses Point" April to October IR£35
Monday–Thursday, IR£45 Friday–Sunday and
bank holidays; November to March IR£30
Monday–Thursday, IR£40 Friday–Sunday and
bank holidays. "Bowmore" IR£15 (9 holes) IR£25 (18 holes).
Telephone: 071 77134

The exhilarating, long, tough "Rosses Point" is a heavenly course in fine weather. When the wind and rain attack from the Atlantic, it's a brute. And it makes few concessions to ladies for whom it is a whopping par 75. The course you see today was laid out in 1928 by the great English golf architect, Harry Colt. The design was largely determined by a dominant feature in the landscape – the huge ridge that rises from the clubhouse and falls steeply to the undulating plain, near sea level, on which 13 of the holes are played. These run roughly north-south through low dunes and ridges. You know what you are taking on from the two uphill opening holes. There is a brief respite on the 3rd, played back downhill. From the high tee you can see out over Sligo Bay. (To your right, below the ridge, you can see the new 9-hole layout, which the club has recently built.) Behind you is the great table mountain, Ben Bulben. Before you, in Sligo Bay, Oyster Island and Coney Island lie close to the shore. (Coney Island, New York, takes its name from here.) The 5th is a great strike from the height of the ridge to the plain beneath. Fill your lungs, open your shoulders and hit fearlessly on this dramatic par 5. The fairway below is generous. But from now on you are at the mercy of the prevailing wind, which blows from west to east across most of the holes. To add to your difficulties, streams come into play on five holes – most dangerously on the 7th (par 4, par 5 for ladies) where a stream crosses the fairway diagonally in front of the green. The 9th – "Cast a Cold Eye" – begins a series of three holes along a narrow promontory in Drumcliff Bay. (The name refers to the epitaph on the grave of the poet WB Yeats in Drumcliff Churchyard almost directly opposite.) As you play back along this promontory on the 11th (par 4) you can see Lissadell House in the woods across the water to your right. A beach cuts in from the right at the 13th (par 3). But don't take too much club, a stream flows behind the well-bunkered green. A stream crosses the fairway at the 14th and the 15th is a long par 4 threaded through dunes. The 17th is the glory of the back nine, and the whole links. There is nothing like it. The fairway climbs through sand dunes to the right and stops abruptly at a deep hollow before turning sharply left to the green near the top of the ridge. The 18th calls for a blind tee-shot over the top of the ridge, and seems almost easy by comparison.

BEYOND THE 18TH GREEN

Between Rosses Point and Erris Head the coastal landscape changes. In County Sligo, farmland runs down to sandy, surfing beaches and low cliffs. Beyond Killala Bay, in County Mayo, high cliffs, caves and sea stacks line the craggy coastline. The high ground near the coast is blanketed with bog.

The landscape around **Sligo Town** (Sligeach – "Abounding in Shells") is dominated by **Knocknarea Mountain** (Cnoc Na Ria – "Hill of the Executions") to the west and **Ben Bulben** (Ben Ghulbain – "Beak Pinnacle") to the north. The Garavogue River flows from **Lough Gill** through the town and into the harbour. This is the landscape that shaped the poet WB Yeats (1865–1939) and his brother, the painter Jack Yeats who said, "Sligo was my school and the sky above it".

Lissadell House

Sligo County Museum, in Stephen Street, **Sligo Town**, has a special section on the Yeats family. (Opening times vary. Telephone: 071 47190). The **Model Arts Centre** in the Mall, houses the **Niland Collection** of twentieth-century Irish art including paintings by Jack Yeats, and that other famous artist of the west of Ireland, Paul Henry. (Open daily 11am–5pm. Telephone: 071 41405)

You can take a three-hour boat tour of places which inspired WB Yeats and hear his poetry recited en route. The "Wild Rose" glass-covered boat makes the round trip from the riverside in **Sligo** along the north shore of lovely, wooded **Lough Gill** past **The Lake Isle of Innisfree** (Inis Fraoigh – "Island of the Heather") to **Parke's Castle** – a seventeenth-century fortified manor – where it stops for a tour. It returns along the south side of the Lough Gill. You can board the "Wild Rose" at either **Parke's Castle** or **Sligo**. (Two sailings daily, June to September. Telephone: 071 64266)

Yeats died in France in 1939 and was buried in Roquebrune on the French Riviera. He was re-interred, as he had wanted, in Drumcliff Churchyard (Droim Chliabh – "Ridge of Baskets") in the shadow of Ben Bulben. His grave has a plain headstone bearing the self-composed epitaph – the last two lines of his poem *Under Ben Bulben*:

> *Cast a cold eye on life, on death*
> *Horseman, pass by.*

The church (C of I) is on the site of a monastery founded by Saint Colmcille in AD574 but the only traces are the stump of a round tower (across the road from the church) and a tenth-century high cross. (Signposted 8km/5miles north of Sligo on the N15.)

WB Yeats often visited Constance and Eva Gore-Booth at **Lissadell House**, which still belongs to the Gore-Booth family. In 1918, Constance, Countess Markievicz, was the first woman elected to the British House of Commons.

Because she belonged to Sinn Fein, then fighting for Independence, she refused to take up her seat at Westminster. She later became the Minister for Labour in the first post-Independence Dail (Parliament). The austere Greek Revival house built in delicately chiselled blocks of Ballisodare limestone overlooks the sea at **Drumcliff Bay**. Count Casimir Markievicz decorated the columns in the dining room with paintings of the gamekeeper, forester, butler and a self-portrait. The housekeeper's column is blank. (Signposted from the N15. Open Monday–Saturday, June to mid-September. Telephone: 071 63150 for opening hours.)

From the N15 a road (signposted) leads up along the foothills of the limestone **Dartry Mountains** (Sléibhte Dhartrái) to lovely **Glencar Lough** (Gleann an Chairthe – "Valley of the Standing Stone"). There is a footpath to the 15metre/49ft Glencar Waterfall, which Yeats wrote about in his poem *The Stolen Child* :

> *Where the wandering water gushes*
> *From the hills above Glen Car...*

A huge cairn 61metres/200ft in diameter, known as Maeve's Mound (Misgaun Medhbh) crowns the summit of **Knocknarea** (603metres/1978ft) above **Strandhill** (An Leathros – "The Half Headland"). It is said to be the burial place of the legendary Queen Maeve of Connacht who went to war with Ulster over a bull. The epic story is told in the longest of the Ulster cycle of stories about the Red Branch warriors and Cú Chulainn – the Taín Bó Cuailgne (The Brown Bull of Cooley). You can climb to the summit from **Knocknarea Mountain** car park (off the R292).

On a limestone plateau, in the shadow of **Knocknarea** lies the largest and earliest megalithic Stone Age cemetery in the world. **Carrowmore** (Ceathru Mhór – "The Great Quarter") is spread out over 4sq km/1.5sq miles of small fields on both sides of a narrow road. The site (signposted from the N4 and R292) was poorly protected until recently and monuments were destroyed by gravel digging. (They were built on a low gravel ridge.) Sixty cairns, dolmens, stone circles and a passage grave remain out of more than a hundred structures. You can wander through the site at any time. The **Carrowmore Heritage Centre** has guided tours in summer. (Open April to October, 9.30am–6.30pm. Telephone: 071 61534)

The **Owenmore River** (Abhainn Mór – "Big River") cascades over a series of rock ledges at **Ballisodare** (Baile Easa Dare – "Waterfall of the Oak") on the N59 from **Sligo** to **Ballina**. Turn left for **Coolaney** (Cúil Mhaine – "Nook of the Thicket") and a scenic detour (26km/16miles) through the **Ox Mountains** (Sliabh Gamh – "Mountain of Storms"). Follow signs for **Ladies' Brae** (244metres/800ft) from where there is a glorious view over **Ballisodare Bay** and **Sligo Bay**, with

Knocknarea and **Ben Bulben** in the background. The road rejoins the N59 near **Skreen** (Scrín – "Shrine").

From the N59 take the R297 to **Easky** (Iascach – "Full of Fish"). Close to the road, about 3km/2miles from the village is a relic of the ice ages – a curiously split rock known as **Finn Maccool's Fingerstone**. You can take a riverside walk from the bridge in **Easky** along the tumbling Easky River to a stony surfing beach. The ruined keep was a fifteenth-century stronghold of the MacDonnells who came as gallowglasses (mercenaries) from Scotland to fight for the O'Dowds who were chiefs in this area. If you look carefully you will see most of the stones on the beach are fossils.

The ruins of **Castle Firbis** stand between the R297and the sea about 3km/2miles north of **Enniscrone**. The MacFirbis family were scribes and historians to the O'Dowds between the fourteenth and seventeenth centuries. Their most famous works of history and genealogy are held in university libraries and in the Royal Irish Academy in Dublin.

Enniscrone (Inis Crabhann – "Island of the Gravel Ridge") on **Killala Bay** is famous for its long, golden strand, backed by the dunes which give the golf course its excitement and splendour. If you have battled through the dunes, or even if you haven't, a hot **Seaweed Bath** at **Kilcullen's Bathhouse** (established 1912) will leave you rested and glowing. (Open daily 1st May to 30th October, 10am–9pm; July/August, 10am–10pm; weekends and bank holidays 31st October to 30th April, 10am–8pm. Telephone: 096 36238)

In the salmon season, fishermen line the banks of the **River Moy** in **Ballina** (Béal an Átha – "Mouth of the Ford"). The Moy (Muaidh – "Stately") is one of the most famous salmon rivers in the world and eight beats in the **Moy Fishery** are within the town boundaries. The ruined Augustinian **Friary** was founded by the O'Dowds in the fifteenth century. The church has a window decorated with sculptures of human heads and an ornamented doorway.

Rosserk Abbey (Ros Eirc – "Wood of Eirc") one of the finest Franciscan foundations in Ireland, stands in a peaceful spot overlooking a small island in the estuary of the River Moy, about 8km/5miles north of **Ballina**. It was founded in 1441 for the third Order of Saint Francis – devout lay members of the church – and burned by the English Governor of Connacht, Sir Richard Bingham, in 1590. The bell tower, nave, south transept, choir and cloister remain. The choir has a double piscina (recessed stone washbowls for sacred vessels) on which are carved angels and a round tower. Animals and angels are carved on the pillars of the arch of the nave and on a pillar to the right of the four-light east window. (Signposted from the R314. Always accessible.)

Sir Richard Bingham also burned **Moyne Abbey** (An Mhaighean – "The Precinct") 2km/1mile further north on the shores of **Killala Bay**. MacWilliam Burke founded it for the Franciscans in the fifteenth century. The cloisters are perfectly preserved. The remains include the nave, choir, side aisle and transept, refectory, dormitories and tower. (Signposted from the R314. You have to walk across some fields.)

A well-preserved eleventh-century **Round Tower** rises above the pretty town of **Killala**, opposite **Bartragh Island** which lies across **Killala Bay** and shelters **Killala** harbour. Round towers were built in monastic settlements as refuges from Viking invaders. They are unique to Irish architecture. The tower is 26metres/84ft tall and 5metres/17ft in diameter. The single doorway is 3.5metres/11ft above the ground. (The doorway was reached by a ladder that was hauled up when the monks were safely inside.) In 1798 French troops commanded by General Humbert landed in Killala Bay in support of the Irish rebellion in that year. Despite an initial victory in County Mayo, he was eventually defeated and the rebellion failed.

Blanket bog covers much of the high ground between **Ballycastle** and the flat land of the **Mullet Peninsula**. Over 5,000 years ago, this land was fertile and was farmed by the earliest inhabitants of the area. By the beginning of the Bronze Age (2000BC) the steadily encroaching bog had covered this farm landscape. It also preserved it. Archaeologists have discovered a well-organised field system under the bog. It is known as the **Ceide Fields** and is one of the world's most extensive Stone Age excavations. The **Ceide Fields Visitor Centre** explains the archaeology, geology, botany and wildlife of the area. (Opening times vary season to season. Closed December to mid-March. Telephone: 096 43325) On the other side of the road, a balcony above the cliffs gives a fine view of the magnificent scenery west from here to **Benwee Head** – 16km/10miles as the abounding sea birds fly. The **Stacks of Broad Haven** (Na Stácaí – "The Stacks") rise 91metres/300ft from the sea 3km/2miles off **Benwee Head** (Beann Bhui – "Yellow Peak"). The area from here to **The Mullet Peninsula** is known as **Erris** (Iorras). It is a **Gaeltacht** (Irish-speaking area).

For a closer view of the **Stacks**, turn right at **Glenamoy Bridge** (Gleann na Muaidhe – "Glen of the Clouds") and make the 26km/16mile detour across the **Annie Brady** bridge to **Portacloy** (Port an Cloiche – "Port of the Stone") where the harbour is surrounded by towering cliffs.

Belmullet (Béal an Mhuirthead – "Sea Loop") is at the end of the narrow strip of land which connects the **Mullet Peninsula** to the rest of County Mayo and separates **Broad Haven** (Cuan an Inbhir – "Harbour of the Estuary") from **Blacksod Bay** (Cuan an Fhoid Dhuibh – "Harbour of the Black Sod"). North of **Belmullet** small lonely roads criss-cross the broad flat land of the peninsula. The main road runs south past blue flag beaches through **Aghleam** to **Blacksod Point**. There are many sites of mythological and historical interest along the way.

The island of **Inishglora**, 1.6km/1mile offshore, is associated with **Saint Brendan the Navigator** (died AD577) who is said to have discovered America a thousand years before Christopher Columbus. A beehive hut dates from the sixth century. **St Brendan's Chapel** dates from the twelfth century. **Inishglora** (Inis Gluaire – "Island of the Voice") is also associated with the legend of the **Children Of Lir** who were turned into swans by their jealous stepmother and doomed to roam the waters of Ireland for 900 years. According to the legend they spent their last 300 years on Inishglora before being released from their spell by the ringing of Saint Patrick's bell. They came ashore from **Inishglora** but, being more than 900 years old, died immediately.

The **Inishkea Islands** (Inis Ge – "Ge's Island") lie further south and further offshore. **Saint Colmcille** founded a monastery on **Iniskea North** in the sixth century. The village on the island was abandoned in 1927 after ten fishermen drowned in a storm. The story is told in the **Heritage Centre** at **Aghleam** (Eachléim – "Horse Leap") where you can also read about the poet **Riscard Bairead** (1740–1819) and his **Hedge School**. (Under the Penal Laws, Catholics were forbidden education and so secret schools were organised in hedges and ditches.) One of his most famous poems "Tarraingt na Mona" (Taking the Turf) poked fun at the local landlord, Major Bingham (an ancestor of Lord Lucan who went missing in England after the murder of his children's nanny.) **Inishkea Charters** do boat trips to the islands. Allow at least three hours for a trip to the **Inishkea Islands** and at least four hours for **Inishglora**. (Telephone: 097 85669)

The road from **Aghleam** loops around **Blacksod Point** and **Fallmore** (An Fál Mór – "Big Cliff") from where there are stunning views of the **Inishkea Islands** and **Achill Island** further south. (The stone circle, like great jagged teeth on the headland, is modern.) **Saint Deirbhle's Well** is near the sixth-century ruins of her church by a pretty stream, lined with irises, that runs down through small fields to the sea. The saint's grave, **Deirbhle's Bed**, is stony. Tradition says grass doesn't grow on the grave of a saint.

TOURIST INFORMATION

Sligo Tourist Information Centre: Aras Reddan, Temple Street, Sligo
Telephone: 071 61201
Westport Tourist Information Centre: The Square, Westport, Co. Mayo
Telephone: 098 25711

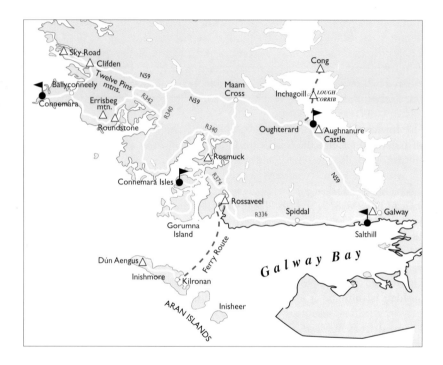

*(Golf Courses: Galway, Oughterard, Connemara Isles and Connemara –
Ballyconneely)*

*Distances: Galway to Oughterard 27km/17miles; Oughterard to Clifden
51km/32miles (N59); Galway to Lettermore 46km/29miles (R336); Oughterard to
Lettermore 48km/30miles; Clifden to Ballyconneely (golf course) 15km/9miles;
Lettermore to Rossaveel 10km/6miles.*

Galway is a lively university city with a rich cultural life and an interesting
history. It began as a fishing village – salmon still fight their way up the Corrib
River through the city – but by the fourteenth century had developed a lucrative
sea trade with continental Europe. You can see traces of Galway's rich mediaeval
past in the narrow streets leading from the port to the city centre. Connemara

has no clear definition. In the language of tourism it means everywhere west of Galway city. More accurately, it is the region between the western shores of Lough Corrib, the Atlantic and Killary harbour. The name conjures up a landscape of bare mountains, peaty lakes, islands and rocky inlets of the sea constantly altered by fleeting clouds across the sky. The light plays particularly on the Twelve Pins – a cluster of rounded peaks about 600metres/2000ft high. If you can see them you are definitely in Connemara. Even if you can't see them you may still be in Connemara. The weather in the far west of Ireland is famously unpredictable.

GALWAY

18 holes – par 70 (5816metres/6462yards)
At Salthill, 5km/3miles west of Galway city on the R336 to Spiddal.
Green Fees: IR£20 weekdays, IR£25 weekends.
Telephone: 091 522033

> *"Dr MacKenzie is one of the real artists in golf course construction. In years to come visitors will probably come from overseas to see the works of the master. 'This is a genuine MacKenzie bunker' they will be told, and the visitors will view it with a reverence with which we at the present day view a Holbein or a Rembrandt."*
> (Golfing magazine, October 1923)

This is a mature parkland course of great character with superb views across Galway Bay. The first four holes are links, then the course moves inland to higher ground. Golf has been played here since 1895 and the present 1923 layout was the work of the famous doctor turned golf architect, Alister MacKenzie, whose treatise Golf Architecture is regarded as a classic. (He designed Cypress Point and Augusta National, in the United States, and Alwoodly in England.) Christy O'Connor Senior, the professional who put Ireland on the world golf map, was born within a wedge shot of the 7th tee and learned the game as a caddy here. In late spring and summer, the course glows golden with gorse. There is a long carry from the 15th over mounds of it. The first four holes by the sea are reached by a tunnel under the coast road and the 1st hole skirts a small lake with swans. You come back through the tunnel to complete the first nine, which loops back to the clubhouse. The back nine climbs to wonderful views of the Aran Islands and the Burren on the other side of Galway Bay in County Clare. The layout is tight and sometimes confusing. (The ladies' tee on the 12th is very far forward and the 15th tee is hard to find without clear directions.) Shorter hitters will find the course testing enough. Long hitters can probably leave the driver in the bag. But they will need to be accurate. The course is well bunkered, the inland fairways are lined with trees, and some greens are tiered. Winds from the sea can make club selection difficult. This is a friendly course and visitors are made very

Oughterard Golf Course

welcome. But expect to play at a brisk pace. The club has 1,200 members and in the summer holiday season about 300 golfers play the course every day.

OUGHTERARD
18 holes – par 71 (6005metres/6672yards)
2km/1.5miles east of Oughterard on the N59 to Galway.
Green Fees: IR£20, IR£30 per couple.
Telephone: 091 552131

Oughterard golf club, near the shores of Lough Corrib, has a well-founded reputation for friendliness. Patrick Merrigan (Tulfarris, Woodenbridge, Faithlegg, Water Rock) has recently remodelled the course. He has added three deep ponds by digging into the peat around the 9th, 10th and 11th holes. This means they are natural bog lakes in which the water rises and falls naturally. They don't have the PVC lining which is sometimes visible on man-made lakes. He is also encouraging the club to remove some of the evergreens, which line the fairways and surround some of the greens, and replace them with native hardwood trees. (Evergreens can slow the drying of greens in winter by blocking

the wind.) Oughterard is set in lush, tranquil, wooded parkland, bounded by stone walls, with views across the untamed countryside – gorse and hawthorn-filled fields rising to craggy hills beyond. In late spring and early summer when the gorse and hawthorn are in bloom, the mingled scent of pine and blossom is carried everywhere on the breeze. The 2nd demands a drive to a typically tree-lined, generous fairway. But the well-bunkered green is over a hill, and the length of this par 4 (375metres/410yards) can tempt you to over-hit and land in the trees. Nor can you see the green from the 8th tee, set back in the trees. Neither can you see the curve in the stone wall on this double dogleg that tempts you to cut corners. Don't. The walls, trees, bunkers and out-of-bounds are there to trap you. Play it as the par 5 it is and you'll be fine. The 9th (par 3) over the first of the ponds, calls for a long and accurate strike to a green protected by bunkers on both sides. The 13th – a pretty par 3 through an avenue of trees to a well-defended green – is a particular favourite with the members. The 16th (par 4) along a boundary wall, seems longer than its 394metres/431yards because it's usually played into the wind. The 18th is a dogleg right, the green is tucked in behind pines and copper beeches. The greens are subtly contoured and not as straightforward as they look. Trees, shrubs and lush grass in the rough punish those who stray from the wide fairways. Large windows on three sides of the bar in the clubhouse overlook the course.

CONNEMARA ISLES

9 holes – par 71 (4770metres/5300yards)
29km/18miles from Oughterard. N59 to Maam Cross then R336 to Costelloe and R374 to Bealdangan. The golf course is on Annaghvane Island connected to Bealdangan by a causeway.
Green Fee: IR£10.
Telephone: 091 572498/154

Connemara Isles is an absolute charmer. It must be one of the most glorious spots on earth for a game of golf. When the three O'Loinsigh (Lynch) brothers – a vet, a guard (policeman) and a teacher – inherited the family farm on Annaghvane Island in the heart of the Connemara Gaeltacht (Irish-speaking area) they decided to develop it as a golf course. The thatched farm cottage that is now the clubhouse adds to its charm. On a fine day, when the sun sparkles on the sea, it's joy to walk the course, admire the views and never mind the score. On a cold and rainy day, you can look forward to a hot whiskey beside the open turf fire in the clubhouse. The course is laid out on Annaghvane Island and on a tiny island connected to Annaghvane by two causeways. It's a short course that, nevertheless, demands some long hits. The 3rd (par 3) requires a long carry across an ocean inlet to an island green. There is no dropping zone. (The scene in Tin Cup where Kevin Costner refuses to lay up and insists on hitting a 7-iron across a lake comes to mind. He got across on the seventh attempt.) With the wind behind, a big hitter could take a wedge. Wind against, and it's a driver you'll be pulling out of the bag. The 4th is played along the smaller island with the sea on both sides. The 5th requires another long carry back to Annaghavane and uphill to the green. You have been warned. This is exhilarating golf, but shorter hitters might prefer to play Stableford. Look out for seals by the bridge connecting the golf course to the mainland. There are blackberries in autumn and golden gorse in the spring. In the summer it's light from 5am until after 10pm. In the winter, it's dark at four. But that still leaves time for a round of golf. The course is never waterlogged and frost is rare.

CONNEMARA (BALLYCONNEELY)

(27 holes) 18 holes – par 72 (6579metres/7200yds)
Signposted at Ballyconneely, 9km/5.5miles from Clifden.
Green Fees: IR£35 May to September, IR£30
April and October, IR£22 rest of the year.
Telephone: 095 23502

Connemara, or Ballyconneely as it is sometimes called, has recently added another 9 holes allowing the club to direct players to any two out of three loops of nine. Each loop has different characteristics. The original 18, laid out by Eddie Hackett, begins on flattish ground – the principal feature being the outcrops of rock that dot every hillside and field in Connemara. The wind is always in play; the rough less innocuous than it looks. But the fairways are generous and the straight hitter shouldn't have too much difficulty on the first nine, unless the magnificent views on the 7th (par 5) are too much of a distraction. The 12th – a long, uphill, into-the-wind par 4 to a plateau green defended by bunkers – begins a sequence of marvellous holes in the dunes. The 13th (par 3) demands a huge carry over mounds of rough, the ladies' tee, and the bunkers set into the slope up to the green. A little strip of fairway in front of the green runs down into rushes and an iris-filled pond. The hillside behind is all rocks. (There is the luxury of a lavatory to the left of the ladies' tee.) From the high 14th tee you have a bird's-eye view over the course, the Atlantic and the Twelve Pins. The green on this par 5 is on a platform, which rises on the right of the fairway and has deep bunkers in its steep front slopes. Mounds line the right-hand side of the fairway on the 15th (par 4). The green is tucked into the hillside, surrounded by a sea of marram grass. You have a long carry to the fairway from the windswept 16th tee. You can see a menacing bunker, but not the stream in front of the green. This crosses the fairway in front of the green on the 9th hole of the new layout as well. But most of the new holes lie outside the boundary of the original 18 holes. They begin along the rocky shoreline and are reached through a tunnel under the road. The fairway on the 1st (par 4) slopes to the right, then narrows and bends to the left around mounds. The 2nd (par 3) calls for a very long carry from the back tees across mounds and hollows to the green up on a headland. Then begins a series of six par 4s. The course turns away from the shore, but towards water in the shape of a stream that meanders in front of the 3rd tee, along the left boundary of the fairway, in front of the green and then into a lake. Men drive over the lake and waving bulrushes at the 4th. In general, the new nine are more interesting and challenging than the front nine on the original links. The combination of the new holes and the old back nine promises much.

BEYOND THE 18TH GREEN

Galway golf club is in the long-established seaside resort of **Salthill** (Bothar na Trá – "Strand Road"). Near the entrance to the club are a beach and jetty with diving boards – a very pleasant and popular place to swim. From here you can drive, take a bus, or walk along the 3km/2miles promenade to **Galway City** (Gaillimh – "Stony River").

Traces of the mediaeval city founded by the Anglo-Norman de Burgo family in the thirteenth century are still visible and best seen on foot. Gargoyles decorate the exterior of sixteenth-century **Lynch's Castle** (which now houses a bank) on Shop Street. Legend says Christopher Columbus prayed in the collegiate **Church of St Nicholas** (C of I). It was founded in 1320 and is the largest mediaeval church in Ireland. The fifteenth-century west doorway is particularly fine. The **Spanish Arch** is a fragment of the mediaeval city walls, which had 14 towers. The gardens in **Eyre Square** are dedicated to John F Kennedy who was given the Freedom of the City when he visited Galway before his assassination in 1963. The steel sculpture in the square is based on the sails of traditional Galway fishing boats, known as **Galway Hookers**. There is also a statue of the writer **Padraic O'Conaire** (1883–1928) who pioneered a revival of literature in Irish. The **Gaeltacht** (Irish-speaking area) begins just a few miles west of Galway. You can hear Irish and English (and a good half dozen other European languages) spoken in the city streets. At the **Bridge Mill** you can watch the world go by and the salmon line up to leap the weir on their way upriver.

From Galway city you can go to **Connemara** (Conmaicne Mara – "Conmaicne Tribe of the Sea") on the N59 along the shores of **Lough Corrib**, or on the R336 along the coast through **Spiddal** (An Spidéal – "Hospital"). The striking **St Eanna's Church** in the Celtic Revival style in Spiddal (1904) was designed by William Scott.

The area around **Leitir Mór** (Lettermore Móir – "Big Hillside") and **Bealdangan** (Béal an Daingin – "Mouth of the Stronghold") is known as **Na hOileáin** ("The Islands"). The causeway connecting this series of islands to the coast was built in 1890.You can drive through **Leitir Mór** and **Leitir Mealláin** (Lettermullan – "Hillside of Meallán") through a maze of stone walls and small fields to the edge of the Atlantic.

You can make a day trip to **Inis Mor** ("Great Island") the largest of the three **Aran Islands** from **Ros A'Mhil** (Rossaveal – "Peninsula of the Sea-monster"). Passenger ferries (not cars) make the 18km/11mile crossing daily to **Cill Rónáin** (Kilronan – "Ronan's Church") the chief town and port on **Inis Mór**. The crossing takes 40 to 50 minutes. On the island you can walk, bicycle, take a mini-bus or pony and trap to the finest and most dramatically situated pre-Christian stone forts in Europe – **Dún Aengus** – on the edge of a sheer cliff rising out of the Atlantic. There are three (formerly four) semi-circular defensive walls in turn defended by a chevaux de frise – thousands of sharp limestone rocks set at various angles. The inner fort contains terraces, stairways and wall chambers. The view is magnificent. There are three other stone forts on **Inis Mór** as well as ecclesiastical ruins from the sixth century when St Enda made **Inis Mór** the Island of the Saints. The **Heritage Centre** in **Cill Rónáin** explains the traditions and culture of the islands. (Open daily Easter to September. Telephone: 099 61355)

On the R336 to **Maam Cross** turn left on to the R340 for **Teach An Piarsaigh** ("Pearse's Cottage") built near **Rosmuc** (Rosmuck – "Headland of Pigs") by **Padraig Pearse**, leader of the 1916 Easter Rising. The execution of Pearse and his fellow fighters by the British authorities swung most of the population of Ireland

Opposite page: Clifden

behind the rebels. The house, where Pearse wrote poems and plays, is now a museum. (Open daily, June to September 9am–6.30pm. Telephone: 091 574292)

A road from the square in **Oughterard** (Uachtar Ard – "Upper Height") leads to the shores of **Lough Corrib** (Loch Coirib – "Lake Of Oirbse"). You can swim from the small jetties, which dot the shoreline close to the town. After about 13 km this road ends at the **Hill Of Doon** (Dún – "Fort") from where there are stunning views of the north-eastern arm of Lough Corrib, the largest island in the lough – **Inchagoill** – and the mountains of **Connemara** in the distance. You can take a 90-minute cruise to **Inchagoill** (Inis an Ghaill – "Island of the Devout Stranger") or a longer cruise to **Cong** (Conga – "Isthmus") on the far side of the lough. (May to September, departures 11.45am for Cong and Inchagoill, 2.45pm for Inchagoill only. Telephone: 091 46029)

Inchagoill has a fifth-century church, and a reconstructed twelfth-century church. But perhaps the most interesting feature on this, the prettiest of the islands in **Lough Corrib**, is the **Stone Of Lugnad**, said to be the burial stone of St Patrick's nephew and navigator. The inscription "Lugnad son of Meanbh" in Roman characters may be the oldest Christian engraving in Europe outside the catacombs in Rome. The longer cruise to **Cong** stops at **Inchagoill** and allows two hours in **Cong** before returning to Oughterard. **Cong Abbey** was founded in the sixth century, destroyed by Vikings, rebuilt in the twelfth century by Turlough O'Connor and restored in the nineteenth century. A river that flows underground connects **Lough Corrib** to **Lough Mask**. It can be reached through cave openings such as **The Horses' Discovery** and The Pigeon Hole. (Signposted.) The Quiet Man was filmed in **Cong** in 1951. The **Quiet Man Cottage** was used as a set and displays photos and memorabilia from the film. (Open daily March to November, 10am–6pm.)

Aughanure Castle (Achadh an Iúr – "Field of the Yew") – only a short stroll from **Oughterard Golf Club** – was a stronghold of the O'Flahertys in the fifteenth and sixteenth centuries. Contemporary documents list a household of the O'Flaherty chief and his family, domestic servants, soldiers, a master of horse, a standard bearer, a physician, two judges, a poet, a master of revels, a steward, a tax collector and two bee keepers. The castle was attacked by Sir Edward Fitton during the Elizabethan conquest and later by Cromwell's army. The O'Flahertys were defeated. The castle fell into ruin. The Office of Public Works has sensitively restored it. The six-storey square tower was built on a river island of rock. It has been re-roofed. The surrounding defensive walls have been conserved, along with a circular guardhouse with a cupola roof. Only one wall of the separate banqueting hall remains. Its windows are decorated with fifteenth-century floral decorative stone carving. It was built over the fast flowing river and in the castle's heyday an unwelcome guest could be tipped into the river from a hinged flagstone in the floor of the hall. There is a fine view of Lough Corrib from the top of the tower. (Open daily, June to mid-September; weekends, Easter to 30th October. Telephone: 091 552214)

The N59 from **Oughterard** to **Clifden** through **Maam Cross** traverses the typical Connemara landscape of mountains, peat bog and small lakes that reflect the changing sky. The **Maamturnk Mountains** (Maam Tuirc – "The Pass of the Boar") are on your right. Then the **Twelve Pins** (Na Beanna Beola – "Beola's Peaks") come into view on the right with wooded **Ballynahinch Lough** (Baile na hInse – "Homestead of the Holm") on your left. The **Twelve Pins** dominate the landscape behind the popular and pretty market town of **Clifden** (An Clochán – "The Stepping Stones") at the head of a narrow sheltered bay. Take the **Sky Road** (signposted) from Clifden along the bay and high above the town and the ruined **Clifden Castle**, built in 1815 by the D'Arcy family who gave the town its Georgian character. **Sky Road** circles the peninsula on the western shores of **Clifden Bay**. There are breath-taking sea views all along the 14km/9mile drive.

On the R341 from **Clifden** to **Ballyconeely** (Baile Conaola – "Homestead of Conaola") there's a signpost to the spot where **Alcock** and **Brown** crash-landed in a bog at the end of the first non-stop flight across the Atlantic in 1919. The road from **Ballyconeely** to **Roundstone** is known as the "Brandy and Soda" road because of the intoxicating sea air. On it, back to back on a long, sandy promontory, are two beaches that sparkle with white shell sand – **Gorteen** (Goirtín – "Little Tilled Field") and **Dog's Bay** (Port na Feadoige – "Bay of the Plover"). You can leave the car at **Dog's Bay** and walk around the promontory to **Gorteen**.

Roundstone (Cloch na Rón – "Rock of the Seals") has a pretty, almost land-locked harbour built in the nineteenth century by the Scots engineer, Alexander Nimmo. It lies beneath **Errisbeg Mountain** (Iorras Beag – "Small Promontory") – an easy and rewarding climb. There are superb views over **Dog's Bay** and **Gorteen** below, and over the typically Connemara landscape of small shimmering lakes and the **Twelve Pins**. The R341 rejoins the N59 between **Clifden** and **Galway**.

TOURIST INFORMATION

Galway Tourist Information Centre: Aras Fáilte, Victoria Place,
Eyre Square, Galway
Telephone: 091 563081

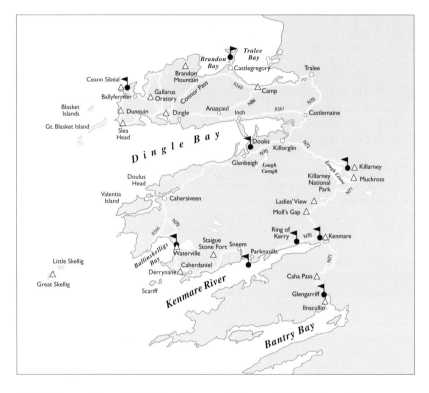

(Golf Courses: Ceann Sibéal, Castlegregory, Killarney, Dooks, Waterville, Parknasilla, Ring of Kerry, Kenmare and Glengarriff)

Distances: Killarney to Killorglin 19km/12miles; Killorglin to Dingle 54km/33miles; Dingle to Ballyferriter (coastal route) 35km/22miles; Killorglin to Waterville 56km/35miles; Waterville to Kenmare 63km/39miles; Kenmare to Killarney 34km/21miles; Kenmare to Glengarriff 27km/17miles.

Killarney, in Ireland's lake district, has been attracting tourists since the eighteenth century. South and west of Killarney, Dingle Bay and Kenmare Bay separate the Kerry peninsulas. The Gulf Stream warms the waters and the climate is mild. Lush vegetation lines the coast. Mountains tower above. At every bend of the road there is a different view of the sea. The view is constantly changing, for the Kerry roads are narrow and twisting. Don't do too much in a day. Savour the splendid scenery both on and off the golf course. Golfers know Killarney and Waterville the world over. But Kerry has some hidden gems as well – all of them in beautiful settings. Glengarriff is only 30 minutes from Kenmare via a spectacular mountain pass, and so has been included with the Kerry courses. You can scarcely believe there is a golf course on the very tip of the Dingle Peninsula – but there is.

CEANN SIBÉAL
18 holes – par 72 (6021metres/6690yards)
Near Ballyferriter on the R559.
Green Fees: IR£25 per round, IR£35 per day, IR£16 early bird (before 8am), IR£12 twilight (after 6.30pm).
Telephone: 066 9156255

Ceann Sibéal is Irish for Sibyl Head – the craggy promontory which rises behind the golf course and overlooks the Atlantic at this most westerly point in Ireland. From the comfortable clubhouse, the course slopes gently towards flatter ground between Ballyferriter Bay on the right and Smerwick harbour – a natural sea inlet – on the left. You can see nearly all the course from the 1st tee in front of the clubhouse. The large island out to sea is Inis Tuaisceart ("Northern Island") – known locally as "An Fear Marbh" (The Dead Man). The jagged point, which seems to be rising from his chest, is actually a lighthouse on another island behind Inishtookert. The smaller rocky island in the bay is Beag Inis ("Little Island"). Mount Brandon, Ireland's second highest mountain, overlooks Smerwick harbour. Behind and to your left are three headlands known as the Three Sisters. This panorama can be enjoyed from everywhere on the course – providing you get a fine day. On the 1st hole – Poll na Cruaiche – you encounter the principal feature of Ceann Sibéal – a fast-flowing stream that weaves across the course and comes into play on ten holes. It flows across the front of the 1st green. The 2nd, Poll an tSeáláin, is a well-defended par 3. The stream is particularly troublesome on the 9th (par 4). Short hitters must aim for the left of the fairway. The stream will catch a too-short drive on the right. The most memorable hole is the 10th – another par 3. It requires an uphill drive to the green tucked into the hillside and mostly hidden by mounds. The prevailing westerly wind blows left to right. You are playing the most westerly golf hole on the most westerly golf course in Europe. The 16th has a blind tee-shot; your second shot must carry the stream and the green slopes steeply. All the signs on the course and in the clubhouse are in Irish. The detailed course guide is in English. June is a good month to play here. The owners of holiday homes in the area who make up a large part of the membership tend to come in July and August making these the busiest months. The course is playable all year round.

CASTLEGREGORY GOLF & FISHING CLUB
9 holes – par 68 (5292metres/5880yards)
3km/2miles west of Castlegregory on the north side of the Dingle Peninsula.
Green Fees: IR£15.
Telephone: 066 7139444

"Do not interfere with the Lakes on the 9th during Natterjack
breeding season (May–July)" (Local rule)

Colonel William Gibson, in his book on early Irish golf courses, found mention of a golf course at Castlegregory in "The Sportsman's' Holiday Guide" 1897 and "The Golfing Annual" 1896/7 – "The Castlegregory course lies between the seashore and one of the best trouting lakes in Kerry. The round.... bristles with hazards in the form of sandhills and bunkers" – "a very fine 18 holes course... It lies along the coast and is quite the first course in the Kingdom of Kerry." The course fell into disuse in 1907 and lay hidden until the late 1980s when it was rediscovered and rescued by Dr Arthur Spring – a doctor turned golf architect like the illustrious Dr Alister MacKenzie (designer of Cypress Point). Arthur Spring has created a nine-hole gem in the dunes between the trout lake – Lough Gill – and Brandon Bay. Wild swans nest in the lakeside reeds along the opening par 5 which curves around the lake to a green protected by the lake and two bunkers. The 6th and 7th are played alongside the beach, to your left, on Brandon Bay. The 7th green juts out into the sea. A stream flows across the 8th/17th fairway and into the lakes, which Arthur Spring created for the Natterjacks, in front of the 9th/18th green. (The Natterjack toad – *Bufo calamita* – is native to Kerry. It has a narrow, yellow stripe running down its back, it crawls quickly instead of hopping and it sings like a drill. You will usually only hear it in the evening or at night in spring and summer. It hibernates in tunnels in the winter.) Castlegregory is a wonderful, natural links with all the best links features – sandhills, springy turf, native bent and fescue grasses. It seems to have a microclimate too. At any rate, when it's raining in other parts of the Peninsula, the sun shines on Castlegregory links and its natural denizen the Natterjack toad. Lucky toad.

RING OF KERRY
There are eight golf courses on the renowned Ring of Kerry. Three of them are in Killarney, the golfing capital of the south west.

KILLARNEY GOLF & FISHING CLUB
"Killeen" 18 holes – par 72 (6474metres/7193yards)
"Mahoney's Point" 18 holes – par 72 (6164metres/6849yards)
"Lackabane" 18 holes – par 72 (6404metres/7116yards)
Green Fees: IR£43 (each course).
Telephone: 064 31034

Perfect parkland golf in a divine setting – that's Killarney. David McIndoe, who manages all three courses here, thinks Killarney is even more beautiful than Loch Lomond. Praise indeed, for David grew up near Loch Lomond. Killarney now offers 54 golf holes – 36 along the shores of Lough Leane, 18 on the new layout which partly overlooks the lake and which is as tough, if not tougher, than Killeen, the championship course. (When the Irish Open was played here in 1991 and 1992, only the winner, Nick Faldo, finished under par.) Which is not to say golfers should be put off playing Killeen. Like all three courses at Killarney, it offers a choice of tees – you don't have to punish yourself. You walk over an arched wooden bridge to the 1st tee. The fairway curves to the right around the lake. There is water on your right all the way to the green. Across the lake, the mountains rise majestically. You say to yourself "don't slice!" At the 3rd (par 3) you hear "lake water lapping in low sounds by the shore" and think of Yeats, and how you must place your ball on the green. To the right, the ground slopes from green to lake. There are trees, and a bunker on the left. The 5th (a long par 4) turning away from the lake and taking you into the park, is the toughest challenge for men. This dogleg right looks innocuous from the tee. But every shot must be perfectly placed and avoid the ditch on the right, the tree on the left and the fiendishly sited greenside bunker. The (par 3) 6th green is surrounded by a stream and has a beautiful backdrop of mountains. You walk through woodland to the very pretty 8th (par 4) in the heart of the park. On the back nine, the 13th (par 4) may be the best hole in the entire complex. Your approach is over a fast-flowing stream in a hollow. Trees and shrubs frame the small, oval-shaped, elevated green. The 17th (par 4) is the ladies' toughest challenge. The fairway slopes steeply to the left before bearing gently right. The approach to the narrow, elevated green is over a pond and stream.

Mahoney's Point is an easier course. It has a tough start. You drive over a pond on the (par 4) 1st. The 2nd is a well-bunkered, long and difficult dogleg – bunkers and trees in the crook. In general, the fairways and greens are generous. But there are a couple of very tricky greens. The 11th is a very long par 4 (par 5 for ladies) to a triple-tiered green, played into the prevailing wind. The 13th green is very hard to hold. The 16th has some of the loveliest views on a course that is always scenic. The 18th (par 3) – played over an inlet – is the most photographed golf hole in Ireland.

Lackabane is a terrific layout (by Donald Steel) in an inauspicious setting between a housing estate and a large factory, but the ground rises behind the factory so there are fine views out over the lakes. Water – two streams and two ponds – adds interest and difficulty on 7 of the 18 holes. The 2nd (par 5) is a great golf hole – a dogleg right, played uphill and around a majestic oak tree which sits in the middle of the rising fairway and determines the shape of your second shot. From the elevated tees on the 4th and 6th there are fine views out over Lough Leane, the mountains and the town. The 6th is a long, tough,

Ceann Sibéal Golf Course

downhill par 4 (433metres/474yards from the blue tees). The fairway slopes right and curves left to the green. Then comes a long par 5 (543metres/594yards from the blue tees). The approach to the green is over a stream. The 11th (par 5) curves around a pond. On the 12th (par 4) you drive over the pond. The 17th demands another drive over water (a stream) to reach the fairway. The 18th is played into the prevailing wind and is cunningly bunkered. As always at Killarney, the greens are beautifully tended, the tees are immaculate. Weekends are particularly busy in May and September – popular months with golf societies in Ireland. But the additional course means you will get tee times, even in the holiday months of July and August.

DOOKS
18 holes – par 70 (5491metres/6010yards)
At Glenbeigh, 6km/4miles from Killorglin.
Green Fees: IR£25.
Telephone: 066 9768205

Dooks is distinguished by being a golf course largely created by its members. When it was expanded (1967–1970) from 9 holes to the present 18, the members did all the work themselves. They designed the holes, moved the earth, dug the bunkers, shaped and laid the greens. Not surprisingly, the club motto is Per Ardua Ad Astra ("through hard work to the stars"). The logo is the natterjack toad, which lives and breeds around the 14th to the 16th holes. Everything about Dooks tells you the members love it and are justly proud. It is beautifully kept. The atmosphere is warm and friendly. There is a sense of anticipation about the 1st (par 4). You don't know what's in store beyond the left-sloping hill you can see from the tee. You reach the crest and see the green below, the sea and mountains behind. There are magnificent views from every part of Dooks, which runs over three sandbanks along a creek in Dingle Bay and has a permanent backdrop of the Slieve Mish Mountains on the Dingle Peninsula and MacGillicuddy's Reeks on the Ring of Kerry. (Dooks is a derivation of the Irish "dumhac" – sandbank.) On the 6th (par 4) a huge arrow tells you this is a tight dogleg left. If your drive isn't well placed you will have a blind second shot uphill to the green. (Dooks shows its thoughtfulness to visitors by being extremely well signposted.) The 10th (par 4) is well named "Hidden Valley". Your tee-shot to the narrow fairway is blind and into the prevailing wind. The 11th (par 4) – a dogleg to the right, along the shore – is one of the most memorable holes. Waves dance on the sea, out-of-bounds, beyond the dunes and palm trees and waving grasses on your left. The 12th is uphill, against the wind, to a tiered, platform green. The small, saucer-shaped and undulating green on the 13th (par 3) is the trickiest of all. But it also has a magnificent 360-degree view of the wonderful scenery that makes Dooks such a pleasure to play. The ponds on the 15th (par 3) and between the 16th and 17th are breeding grounds for the natterjack. And what a finish is the 18th (par 5)! You drive uphill. You get to the top of the slope. The fairway ends at a depression in the ground. The green is hidden behind a ridge that rises like a ring-fort to defend it. You hit blind over the ridge and hope for the best.

WATERVILLE
18 holes – par 72 (6465metres/7184yards)
Signposted from Waterville village.
Green Fees: IR£75, IR£45 November to March and
before 8.30am, Monday–Thursday in summer.
Telephone: 066 9474102

Waterville is firmly established on the golf circuit for visitors from the United States. Mark O'Meara, Tiger Woods and Ernie Els have prepared for the British Open here. The late Payne Stewart was a particularly cherished visitor. His death was keenly felt at the club and in the community. Golf was first played at Waterville in the 1880s when the transatlantic cable was laid to nearby Valentia Island and then to Waterville. To those accustomed only to fair-weather golf, it is salutary to be reminded that in these parts golf was then a winter game, played on the, naturally, shorter winter greens. The Cable Company sustained a 9-hole links for many years but gradually withdrew with the coming of automation. By the 1960s there was no golf at all. This changed when John A Mulcahy chose Waterville to develop his vision of the most testing golf course in the world. He chose Irish architect Eddie Hackett and former US Masters' champion, Claude Harmon, to produce the links that is hugely admired and the favourite of many. This is not a club where the US influence hits you in the face. There are no sculpted flowerbeds, and the only water is the sea around you and the ponds across which you play the 7th (par 3). The modern clubhouse is an architectural masterpiece of tact, which blends almost invisibly into the landscape. The club invests heavily in course maintenance – most evident in the impeccable greens. The 1st hole is innocuous and aptly named "Last Easy". It gives you time to get into your swing and take in the splendid surroundings. The 2nd 3rd and 4th continue around the perimeter of the course – the 3rd a 381metre/417yard par 4 which doglegs into the estuary at the last minute, demanding nerves of steel or great accuracy. The 4th is a heartbreaking par 3 into the prevailing wind. Dunes surround the green; a bunker defends the narrow opening. After that, you'll be glad to open your shoulders on the long (par 5) 5th – 544metres/595yards. (Even from the ladies' tee it's 408metres /447yards. Although this is a course which is generally kind to ladies.) By the 9th you are within earshot of the breakers on the strand. But you don't see the waves until you stand on the elevated tee at the 12th (par 3) – known as "The Mass Hole" because Mass was celebrated secretly in this hollow in the dunes during penal times. Before this, you will have played the sublime "Tranquillity" – a par 5 whose narrow fairway winds through the dunes to a raised green, offering a half-respite from the wind. The last three holes run above and alongside the beach, with shelter provided by thick stands of New Zealand flax (known locally as "Flaggers"). The 16th is a 320metre/350yard par 4. In 1979, Liam Higgins, the club professional had a hole in one here. And it's a blind drive! The 17th has some of the best views on the course and was the chosen burial place of Waterville's founder, John A Mulcahy. The 18th brings you down a line of flaggers to the clubhouse. It is essential to book tee times well in advance. Early and late slots are more available. Take advantage of the reduced green fees and play before 8.30am. Return to breakfast in the clubhouse and take the rest of the day to explore Kerry.

PARKNASILLA
9 holes – par 70 (5520metres/6041yds)
At the Parknasilla Great Southern Hotel, Sneem.
Course open March to November.Green Fees: IR£16 per day.
Reduced rates for hotel residents including IR£30 weekly.
Telephone: 064 45122

Parknasilla golf course is owned and operated by the adjacent hotel, but unlike many hotel courses, it has a considerable history and was often played by the legendary Irish golfer, Jimmy Bruen. The course is laid out in mature woodland, which competes for space with rhododendrons and sub-tropical vegetation, on a hilly promontory overlooking the island-studded sea. If the scenery doesn't distract you, the varied and melodious birdsong will. This is a charming relic of a time when the game was much less commercial. The clubhouse is entirely in keeping – a small wooden building with a verandah. But Parknasilla is not a decaying relic. It is beautifully maintained and not over-played. (There are usually tee times available.) The original 9 holes have been redesigned by Dr Arthur Spring. The course is to be extended to 12 holes and there are plans for a full 18. The 1st (par 4) is followed by a short climb through shrubbery to the elevated 2nd tee for a par 3 (122metres/134yards) with the green close to the rocky shore. There are steps up to the 3rd tee for the only par 5 on the men's card. (The 9th is also a par 5 for ladies.) It's worth walking back to the blue tees set back into the woods for a shot into the natural cleft that shapes this slight dogleg left. The 4th and 5th take you up again to the highest part of the course. There are spectacular views from the 6th (par 4). It requires a very accurate drive to a flat landing area; otherwise you will be scrambling down slopes to play a recovery shot to the hidden green. The 8th (par 4) is a beautiful downhill hole to a green on a promontory surrounded by water. The 9th tee juts out into the sea. From here you have to negotiate mature trees to drive up the ridge, which take you back to the clubhouse. You will enjoy the course even more the second time around.

RING OF KERRY
18 holes – par 72 (6316metres/6923yards)
6.5km/4miles from Kenmare on the N70 "Ring of Kerry".
Green Fees: IR£45 per round.
Telephone: 064 42000

Nothing prepares you for the audacity of Ring of Kerry golf club. You turn off the road along the north shore of Kenmare Bay to make a near vertical ascent to the modern, chalet-style clubhouse. Within a few minutes you have travelled from relative shelter on the shore to complete exposure on the side of a mountain. Ring of Kerry, which opened in 1998, is an astonishing achievement. The natural soil of the top half of the course is bog. The architects brought in sand by the ship-load to create a base for the fairways and greens. The fairways are a mixture of fescue and rye grasses and the greens are creeping bent. They will need continual fertilisation while they establish. The owners believe they will have created a self-sufficent environment in five to ten years. They claim to have installed sufficient irrigation and drainage to be able to offer year-round golf. There can be few tougher environments in which the golf designer's ingenuity has been put to the test. Time will tell. Meanwhile, a severe test of golf has been created. Men are recommended to stick to the forward tees unless they have a handicap of ten or less. The 1st (par 4) heads off uphill, naturally, past a lake to a plateau landing area. To the left is out-of-bounds. To the right a vicious slope down to a stream bounded by gorse and rushes. From here, your second shot is played up across the

Mahony's Point Golf Course

stream to a well-defended green that falls away on all sides. Depressed? Console yourself with the views across Kenmare Bay, dotted with islands, to the Caha Mountains on the Beara Peninsula. This course is no respecter of handicaps. There is water on every hole. But it is not just some grotesque American-style fantasy. The design acknowledges this is a mountainside in Kerry where it rains a lot. The naturally occurring streams have been landscaped and diverted. The 6th (par 4) plays from an elevated tee, down past a lake, to a plateau, not much of which is visible from the tee. A stream cascades down a staircase of rock from the lake as you play your second shot to the green. The 7th (par 3) kicks uphill again before the enormous sweep of the par 5 (461metres/505yards) down the hill and left to a tree-backed green. The second half of the course is played on the lower slopes, right down to the road. It doesn't necessarily make for easier golf. The 11th (a very long par 5 at 560metres/609yards) twists and turns downhill, calling for accuracy with every shot. From the 14th you gradually work your way

back uphill over a series of long par 4s. The 18th (par 3) is played across a lake to a tiered green. It has already been redesigned to make it a little easier to clear the lake and hold the green, and make a very public finish – in full view of the clubhouse – a little less daunting.

KENMARE
18 holes – par 71 (5403metres/6003yards)
Green Fees: IR£25 Monday to Saturday. IR£30 Sundays.
Telephone: 064 41291

Kenmare has recently been extended from 9 to 18 holes and the two halves of the course are quite distinct. The original layout, comprising the 1st to the 5th and the 16th to the 18th, was along the shores of the Kenmare river estuary. The new, inland holes are reached by a short walk across the road. The original nine are charming, with the water in view from every hole. Indeed, it is very much in play on some of them, with the 2nd (par 3) punishing a slice with a watery finish, and the 3rd (par 4) requiring a significant carry over water. This part of the course is mature and very wooded. You emerge from the trees behind the 4th green to see the 5th (par 4) disappear into more woods 183metres/200yds out. In fact the hole is a 90-degree dogleg to the left, the well placed drive revealing a raised green beside the road. The newer holes traverse some hilly former farmland, also blessed with mature trees and a stream that is in play on several of the holes. The trees are already significant hazards, particularly on the tricky 6th (par 4) where a little local knowledge is necessary to ensure a clear shot across the dip to the elevated green. This part of the course has still to mature in golfing terms, but it provides an attractive contrast to the shoreside holes and plenty of aerobic exercise. The 16th (par 4) is another dogleg with a green right by the shore, while the 17th (par 4) calls for another shot across both water and marsh to an elevated green.

Kenmare is relatively short, although three of the newer holes are par 5s. Although no pushover, it will provide a welcome antidote to some of the more demanding courses in the area. This is a beautiful spot where the non-golfer might be just as happy to walk the golf course as drive the roads.

GLENGARRIFF

Across the Kerry border, on the other side of the Caha Mountains, Glengarriff golf course perches on the side of a sheltered bay dotted with tiny, verdant islands.

GLENGARRIFF GOLF COURSE
9 holes – par 66 (4094metres/4477yards)
1.6km/1 mile from Glengarriff on the N71
Green Fee: IR£12.
Telephone: 027 63134

Glengarriff is short, but don't underestimate this charming and tough little course. It is an excellent example of how the game of golf can be adapted to every terrain. In this lush corner of Ireland, where level ground is at a premium, Glengarriff occupies part of a hillside, which tumbles, towards the sea. From every aspect the views are spectacular and ever-changing: down through the vegetation to Bantry Bay and its islands, and back up the hill to the mountains behind. The club has an old-fashioned, genteel air, borne out by the local rule on the men's card (but mysteriously missing from the ladies') "Ball plugged or lying in hoof work, tractor work or rabbit scrape may be dropped out without penalty on consultation with opponent". Like the other uphill holes at Glengarriff, the 1st (par 4) plays a lot longer than its length (296 yards) suggests. It requires a drive from a tee box buried in the bushes, over the 9th green, past the clubhouse towards a green further uphill beside the road. The 2nd is uphill, beside the road, to a plateau green. If you make the green in two (the crosswind can make this a very tough hole) you are doubly rewarded by spectacular views of the bay. You are now at the top of the course, but the 3rd (170 yards, par 3) is another heart stopper. You must drive across a deep gully to a hill behind which lies the green. No quarter is given to ladies (166 yards) but short hitters will be relieved to see a dropping zone by the road. Long hitters need to be accurate. There is dense undergrowth behind the green.   At the 4th (par 4), men drive over rhododendrons, ladies drive over another gully. To the left lie trees and gorse. Reassuringly, the card says out-of-bounds on this hole applies to men only. Downhill at Glengarriff does not mean easier. The 6th (par 5 for ladies) is a downhill roller coaster, falling away left, then right and turning sharply right to a sheltered green. (If you are speculating about reaching the green in one make sure you have the course to yourself.) The 7th takes you back up the hill and is a very steep climb. Rest on the seats at the back of the 7th green and enjoy the magnificent scenery. Unusually, the 9th/18th is rated the most difficult on the course. There is a blind approach to the green. But at least you will have gained some local knowledge for the second time around. The clubhouse nestles halfway down the hill, with views of the bay from the verandah overlooking the 9th/18th green. Put your green fee in the honesty box beside the changing rooms if there is nobody around.

BEYOND THE 18TH GREEN

Killarney (Cill Airne – "Church of the Sloes") town is the most commercialised tourist town in Ireland, but nothing can detract from the beauty of its setting in a lake-filled valley below the highest mountains in Ireland, MacGillicuddy's Reeks. The lakes are contained within **Killarney National Park**. One of the best ways to see the lakes is to hire a boat from fourteenth-century **Ross Castle** about 2.5km/1.5miles southwest of the town. The recently restored castle is on a long wooded peninsula in the lower lake, **Lough Leane** (Loch Léibhinn – "Léibhinn's Lake"). It was a stronghold of the O'Donoghues and is one of the finest castles in Ireland, in an excellent state of preservation. It was the last Irish castle to surrender to the Cromwellians.

The ruins of fifteenth-century **Muckross Abbey** (Mucros – "Pig Grove") are at the foot of the wooded peninsula that separates **Lough Leane** from the middle lake, **Muckross Lake**. The abbey was suppressed during Henry VIII's dissolution of the monasteries in 1542 but the monks continued to live here until they were driven out by Elizabethan soldiers in 1589. The monks returned and remained until the Cromwellians burned the abbey. The 22-arch cloister at the centre of the complex encloses an open court with a giant yew tree in the middle, and has both Gothic and Romanesque arches. Three stairways lead to the monks' quarters.

Muckross House and **Gardens** are the centrepiece of **Killarney National Park**. This is a car-free area and is best explored on foot or in one of Killarney's famous jaunting cars. This is where you will see the famous Arbutus Unedo, the native Killarney strawberry tree – so-called because its fruits resemble strawberries. The Elizabethan-style house in Portland stone was built in the nineteenth century and now houses the **Kerry Folk Museum**. (Gardens always open. House open daily 9am–6pm mid-March to October; 9am–7pm July and August; Monday to Saturday 11am–5pm November to mid-March. Telephone: 064 31440)

If you are making a circuit of the **Ring of Kerry** it is best to travel clockwise to avoid being stuck behind tour buses (which travel anti-clockwise) on the narrow and twisting road.

The **Torc Waterfall** is signposted on the N71 from **Killarney** to **Kenmare**. A woodland path leads to where the crystal waters fall 18metres/60ft through a series of sandstone crags from the **Devil's Punchbowl** high on **Mangerton Mountain** above **Muckross Lake**. There are wonderful views from the winding path that continues above the falls.

Ladies' View at a bend in the road about 10km/6miles from **Killarney** is so-called because Queen Victoria and her ladies-in-waiting were enraptured by the view from here of the **Upper Lake**.

From **Moll's Gap** the road descends to **Kenmare** (Neidín – "Little Nest") a lively town with lots of bars, cafes and restaurants, surrounded by hills, where the Roughty River (Ruachtach – "Destructive (river)") joins the estuary of the **Kenmare River** (Ceann Mara – "Head of the Sea"). You can walk from the square to the **Fáinne Cloiche Neidín** (Kenmare Stone Circle) in a quiet spot near the old bridge above the Finnihy River. This is the largest Bronze Age (2200–500BC) monument in southwest Ireland. The circle is believed to be orientated on the position of the setting sun on the horizon at the solstices. It encloses a boulder dolmen (megalithic chamber tomb).

The N71 from **Kenmare** to **Glengarriff** climbs high above **Kenmare Bay** and tunnels through the **Caha Mountains** before dropping steeply to lovely, sheltered **Glengarriff** (An Gleann Garbh – "Rough Valley") where sub-tropical trees and plants grow right to the edge of **Bantry Bay**. In the harbour, on **Garinish Island** (Gar Inis – "Rough Island") is one of the most famous and beautiful gardens in Ireland – **Ilnacullin**. The island belonged to the British War Office who built a martello tower as a defence against an invasion by Napoleon. In 1910 the island was bought by Mr and Mrs Annan Bryce who set about transforming it into the exquisite Italian garden, wild garden and walled garden you see today. They brought over the English architect, Harold Peto, to design the Italian garden, which remains the centrepiece of the island garden, linked to the wild garden and the walled garden by architecture and planting. The garden was given to the Irish Nation in 1953. (Open daily March to October. Times vary. Last landing one hour before closing. Telephone: 027 63040)

Parknasilla (Pairc na Saileach – "Willow Field") is a well-known beauty spot on the N70 **Ring of Kerry**. The **Great Southern Parknasilla** has a fine collection of contemporary Irish art – part of a collection built up by the Great Southern Hotels Group. There are paintings and sculptures by Gerard Dillon, Nora McGuinnes, Nano Reid, Camille Souter, Kenneth Webb and many others.

Staigue Prehistoric Fort (Stéig – "Rocky Ledge") standing 152metres/500ft between two mountain streams at the head of a quiet valley, is one of the most perfect and atmospheric stone forts in Ireland. The massive dry-stone rampart surrounds an area 27metres/90ft in diameter. The interior is reached via a long passage covered with slabs. Ten flights of cross-wise steps in near perfect condition indicate significant building skills. (Signposted.)

Derrynane House was the home of the politician **Daniel O'Connell** (1775–1847) known as "The Liberator" for winning Catholic Emancipation in 1828. He brought millions on to the streets in Ireland to demonstrate peacefully against the Act of Union of Great Britain and Ireland (to no avail). The house is now a museum containing many of his possessions and showing a video about his life. He came from an old Catholic land-owning family who had managed to hold on to their estate. His aunt, Eibhlín Dhubh Ní Chonaill, wrote the famous "Lament for Arthur O'Leary", her husband, killed when he refused to sell his horse to the High Sheriff of Cork. (Open May to September, Monday–Saturday 9am–6pm, Sunday 11am–7pm. October and April, Tuesday–Sunday 1pm–5pm. Telephone: 066 75113)

The **Skellig Islands** (Na Scealaga – "Rock Splinters") rise up out of the Atlantic beyond **Ballinskelligs Bay** (Baile an Sceillig – "Homestead of the Rocks"). **Little Skellig** is a gannet sanctuary. You can see the gannets diving vertically from great heights into the sea if you make the two-hour boat trip to **Skellig Michael** where monks endured a harsh existence between the sixth and twelfth centuries. From the landing site, 670 steps ascend to a terraced ledge near the summit of the island. Here are the perfectly preserved beehive cells of the monks. How did they carve the steps and make the cells of corbelled stone, the stone crosses, and the oratories? How did they live in such an inhospitable place? Go if you can, and wonder. Choose a calm day. The crossing can be rough. (Boat trips from **Waterville**, **Caherdaniel** and **Valentia Island** advertised locally.)

Waterville (An Coireán – "The Little Whirlpool") lies on a narrow stretch of land between **Ballinskelligs Bay** and **Lough Currane** (Corrán – "Crescent

Place"). At the lovely upper end of the lake, is **Church Island** with the ruins of a sixth-century oratory said to have been built by Saint Finian.

From **Cahirsiveen** (Cathair Saidhbhín – "Saidhbhín's Stone Fort") onwards, the sea views are of **Dingle Bay** and across to the mountains on the **Dingle Peninsula**. The former Royal Irish Constabulary police barracks now houses a **Visitor Centre** which tells the history of the town and surrounding area. The lofty, turreted building (burned to a shell in the War of Independence) is said to have been intended for the Northwest Frontier of India, but the plans were mistakenly sent to Ireland. It's a good story, but it's not true. (The same legend is attached to many former barracks in Ireland.) The architect of these imperial barracks liked what he called the "Schloss" style and used it all over the Empire.

The **Kerry Bog Village** at **Glenbeigh** recreates the lives of bog-dwellers in the eighteenth and nineteenth centuries. From **Caragh Lake** (Loch Cárthaí – "Lake of the Caragh") there are fine views of **Magillicuddy's Reeks** and **Carrantuohill** (Corrán Tuathail – "Inverted Crescent") Ireland's highest mountain, in the distance.

The **Ring of Kerry** ends at **Killorglin**, on the **River Laune** (Leamháin – "Elm (river)").

THE DINGLE PENINSULA

In this Gaeltacht (Irish-speaking area) majestic mountains, small green fields, white strands, rocky outcrops and islands in the Atlantic are dotted with relics of Ireland's early Christian and pre-Christian past – Ogham stones, tiny corbelled churches, clochans, stone circles and wedge tombs. Spectacular mountain roads cross the peninsula. A scenic corniche road curls around the coast.

The road along the south of the peninsula has lovely views (weather permitting) across **Dingle Bay** to the mountains on the **Ring of Kerry**. The immense strand at Inch (Inse – "Water Meadow") stretches for 6.5km/4miles along the coast where a sand spit creates shallows and almost cuts off **Castlemaine Harbour** from the rest of the bay.

The town of **Dingle** (An Daingean – "The Fortress") was once a walled town, as its name suggests. It had a prosperous trade with continental Europe in the Middle Ages. Today it's a busy, brightly painted fishing port, lively and popular with visitors all year round. It's home to one of Ireland's most famous visitors, the dolphin **Funghi**. There are regular daily boat trips from the harbour to visit **Funghi** out in the bay. You can even swim with him. (Telephone: Swimming trips – 066 9151967. Boat trips – Dingle Boatmen 066 9152626)

The drive around **Slea Head** on the R559 at the tip of the peninsula is one of the most spectacular in the country with views of the **Ring of Kerry Mountains** on the far side of **Dingle Bay** and the **Blasket Islands** off **Slea Head** in the wild Atlantic.

In the townland of **Fahan** (Fán – "Slope") about 5km/3miles west of beautiful **Ventry Strand** (Fionntrá – "White Strand") there are over 400 beehive huts, souterrains and standing stones. Most of them date from the early Christian period (fifth to eighth century). As stone is plentiful and wood is scarce on this wild coast, some have been built more recently by local farmers as storehouses. They have the same unmortared stone construction and conical shape. **Doonbeg Fort** (Dún Beag – "Small Fort") on the other side of the road, is surrounded on three sides by the Atlantic. It is pre-Christian and dates from between 400 and 50BC. An underground passage (souterrain) leads from the inside to the entrance.

At **Slea Head** (Ceann Sléibhe – "Head of the Mountain") you are at the tip of the peninsula from where there are magnificent views of the group of offshore islands known as **The Blaskets** (Na Blascadodaí) separated from the mainland by the, often rough, Atlantic waves. (At the point in the road where you catch your first sight of the **Blasket Islands** there is a rock called Carraig na nDeoir ("Rock of the Tears"). When islanders emigrated to the United States, this was their last glimpse of home before the road took them to Dingle and then to Cork.) It was a hard life for the islanders, yet they made an enormous literary contribution to Ireland. The islanders finally abandoned **Great Blasket** in 1953. **The Blasket Centre** at **Dunquin** (Dún Chaoin – "Smooth Fort") tells the islands' story and features accounts of island life written by **Peig Sayers**, **Tomas O'Crohan** and **Maurice O'Sullivan**. (Open Easter to October. Telephone: 066 56371) You can visit the islands from **Dunquin Harbour**. It is reached by a perilously steep path down the cliffs that surround the tiny harbour. Currachs (traditional open fishing boats made of tarred hide stretched over wooden frames) are drawn up along the bottom of the path and along the pier. Currachs are made at **Ballydavid** (Baile Dhaith – "David's Homestead") on the north side of the peninsula on **Smerwick Harbour**.

If you have time to visit only one site when you play **Ceann Sibéal** golf course, make it **Gallarus Oratory** (Gallaras). This tiny, perfectly symmetrical church of corbelled stone stands in a field not far from the R559. It is as dry and solid today as it was in the eighth century. The corbel system of building is to place horizontally laid stones which jut inwards, one above the other, to form what is called a false arch. The system was first applied in Ireland nearly 5,000 years ago in the construction of prehistoric burial chambers. The dry stones of **Gallarus** fit together so neatly that not a drop of rain has penetrated in a millennium. It is shaped like an upturned boat. There is a door in the west wall and a window in

Currach and sheep, Coumeenoole, Slea Head

the east wall, facing Jerusalem, according to tradition. (Signposted. Always accessible.)

Kilmalkedar Church (Cill Maolchéadair – St Maolcheadair's Church) is one of the best surviving examples of Irish Romanesque architecture. It dates from the twelfth century and the roof may originally have been corbelled, like the oratory. The **Alphabet** stone near the chancel doorway is carved with both **Ogham** and

Roman characters. There is an **Ogham Stone** in the graveyard. (Ogham is a rune-like alphabet dating from about 300BC. It is the earliest known form of writing in Ireland.)

A scenic road from A**ughils** (Eochaill – "Yew Wood") through the **Slieve Mish Mountains** (Sliabh Mis – "Mountain of Mis") crosses the peninsula by the foot of **Caharconree Mountain** (Cathair Con Raoi – "Stone Fort of Cúrí") to **Camp** (Com – "Camp"). The stone fort high up (624metres/2050ft) on an inland promontory is the highest in Ireland and is associated with the legend of **Cú Chulainn** (The Hound of Ulster) who killed Cúrí the King of Munster and carried off his queen, **Blanaid**.

The seaside resort of **Castlegregory** (Caisleán Ghriaire – "Gregory's Castle") is at the head of a flat spit of land which reaches out into the Atlantic between **Tralee Bay** and **Brandon Bay** and includes **Lough Gill** (Loch Gile – "Bright Lake") – a trout lake and bird sanctuary. On the largest of the **Magharee Islands** (Machairí – "Flat Places") off the tip of the peninsula, are the remains of a monastic settlement with beehive huts and two oratories.

The road from **Castlegregory** to **Dingle Town** is over the spectacular **Connor Pass** (An Chonair – "The Path"). It is one of the highest mountain passes in Ireland and the rapid climb should only be attempted in fine weather. From the top of the pass you can see over lakes and valleys to **Dingle Bay** to the south, **Brandon Bay** and **Brandon Mountain** to the north. A truly impressive sight.

TOURIST INFORMATION

(Cork–Kerry Tourism)
Killarney Tourist Office: Beech Road, Killarney
Telephone: 064 31633
Dingle Tourist Information Centre: Telephone: 066 9151188
(March to October)
Kenmare Tourist Information Centre: Telephone: 064 41233
(April to October)

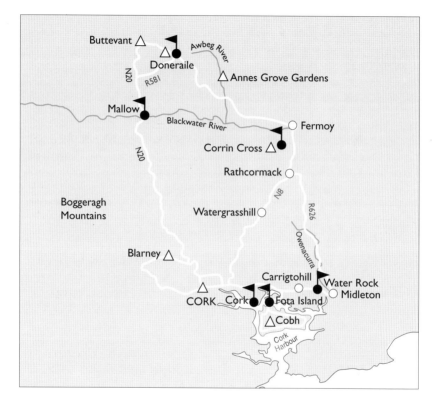

(Golf Courses: Cork, Fota Island, Mallow, Doneraile, Fermoy and Water Rock)

Distances: Cork to Mallow 34km/21miles; Cork to Fermoy 40km/25miles; Mallow to Doneraile 14km/9miles; Cork to Midleton 22km/14miles; Mallow to Fermoy 31km/19miles; Fermoy to Lismore 26km/16miles.

Rich farmland, rolling hills and quiet river valleys with fine old houses and castles, characterise this region. The River Blackwater flows from west to east across the county, through the market towns of Mallow and Fermoy, before turning south towards the sea. The Owenacurra River flows south through a wooded valley to Cork harbour. There are three islands, linked by causeways, in Cork harbour – Little Island, Fota Island and Great Island. East and north of Cork city are some of the loveliest, long-established parkland courses in Ireland. And some fine new courses as well.

CORK
18 holes – par 72
On Little Island, signposted from the N25 east of Cork city.
Green Fees: IR£45 weekdays Monday to Thursday.
IR£50 weekends and bank holidays.
Telephone: 021 353451

> *"Please do not hit your ball if horses are approaching."*
> (Sign at the 4th tee.)

Cork golf club, founded in 1888, is one of Ireland's senior clubs and earns further respect from the long line of champions who have played here. The foremost of these was James Bruen who represented Great Britain and Ireland in their first ever Walker Cup victory in 1938 as an 18-year-old and later won the British Amateur Championship at Birkdale. Respect is also due to the magnificent (and substantially unchanged) layout conceived by Dr Alister MacKenzie in the 1920s when the main tool for course construction was the shovel.

The round begins at a busy junction in front of the clubhouse. The 1st heading uphill into the park, the 14th finishing to the left, the 18th to the right, and the 15th tee-shot driving across the 14th green in front of the 1st tee. A recipe for mayhem at a lesser course, but merely the scene of well-mannered manoeuvres at Cork.

The 1st (340metres/372yards – par 4) requires a drive between trees, nothing too difficult, but your second had better be properly struck to avoid the bunkers to left and right and get to the raised green at the top of the hill. On the 2nd tee (par 5), take a look at your surroundings. The land falls away towards Lough Mahon (at the entrance to Cork harbour) on your right. In the distance is Great Island. This is an extremely peaceful spot. But there are glimpses all around of the industries – old and new – and the shipping on which the city's prosperity was built. Before you on the 2nd tee (par 5) lies a wooded ravine across which you must drive to a fairway sloping gently to the right. (You need to drive long and accurately to score well at Cork.) The 4th (par 4) along the shoreline requires another long carry over a rocky beach to the fairway. At the 5th (par 5) you drive over what seems like acres of gorse, wild roses and honeysuckle. The sea is to the right, and out-of-bounds. Then Cork's famous quarry comes into play. Much of the site for the course was formerly a limestone quarry (which means the course drains swiftly in wet weather). MacKenzie's brilliance was to lead the holes over, through and round this considerable obstacle in a way that seems entirely natural. The tantalising 6th (par 4) calls for a blind drive through a narrow gap with only the high quarry walls in view. The 7th, 8th and 9th are played within the quarry (two excellent par 3s and a tough par 4), with the 10th (374 metres – par 4) taking you out and back down to the shore. From here you climb up into the parkland on the (par 5) 11th (454metres/496yards) where Seve Ballesteros drove 332metres/363yards in 1983. A Spanish chestnut marks the spot. The 13th asks for another long drive over an extraordinarily deep gully to a well-protected green. Then you sweep down to the clubhouse on the 14th to play the parkland holes that complete the round. Don't imagine these are an anti-climax. The short 16th (par 4) requires two accurate shots – the first over a bank of gorse – to make par. The 17th has a 160metre/175yard carry to a sharply sloping fairway with out-of-bounds on the left. You will want to play Cork again and again. It feels like a links course. The greens are fast and true. The rough is abundant with wild flowers, honeysuckle, roses, sea holly, and sweet-smelling gorse. It's peaceful, idiosyncratic and above all, a real test of golf.

FOTA ISLAND
18 holes – par 71 (6329metres/6927yards)
On Fota Island, signposted from the N25 east of Cork city.
Green Fees: IR£45 April to November, Monday–Thursday; IR£35 November to March; IR£55 April to November, Friday–Sunday and bank holidays; IR£45 November to March;IR£55 Christmas period.
Telephone: 021 488 3700

The course lies on the northern shore of Fota Island, one of the larger islands in Cork harbour. It forms part of the Fota Island estate, the attractive clubhouse having previously been the stable block. The first five holes are played in a wide circle of bluebell-filled woodland. As you make your way up the sweeping dogleg 1st (par 4) to the highest point on the course, you will see the huge parkland in which the course is set and understand why it is tranquil, so close to the city. You get your first taste of water when you pitch across the lake on the 3rd (par 3) to a promontory green. You can hear the cries of the waterfowl, or perhaps something more exotic from the nearby wildlife park. Fota doesn't really show its teeth until the 6th (par 4) – a hole with a half-hidden wall crossing it, very much in play. Another wall is the boundary of the estate from the harbour behind the green, gracefully framed by Scots pines. The designer, Jeff Howes, throws the book at you at the 8th (par 4). Look at the lovely stands of trees nearby, and the view back down to the water. Ahead you can see only bunkers at the apex of this dogleg left. There seems to be no way past. Behind the bunkers, a rock-lined stream crosses the fairway as the hole climbs up to a green protected by bunkers and a lake. Young trees line the fairway left and right. The 9th (par 4) reveals a gentle descent to the clubhouse, then it's back down to the waterside for a wonderful series of holes around a large pond populated with ducks and swans.

Cork Golf Course, Little Island

Enjoy, in particular, the 13th (par 3) where you'll need to keep your shot under the wind and out of the water to score. From here you've a demanding climb up the (par 4) 14th (where you may discover, too late, a hidden pond just short of the green on your right). Several beautiful tree-lined holes follow, with a majestic finish down the (par 5) 18th to the promontory green in the pond in front of the clubhouse.

MALLOW
18 holes – par 72 (5960metres/6523yards)
Signposted to the right on the road from Mallow to Kilavullen.
Green Fees: IR£20 weekdays, IR£25 weekends and bank holidays; early bird (before 10am March to mid-May and mid-August to October, before 9am mid-May to mid-August) IR£12 including soup and a sandwich.
Telephone: 022 21145

Mallow is one of those courses where the early bird catches the worm – in this case a bargain price of IR£12 on a beautifully maintained, challenging championship course with soup and a sandwich thrown in to revive you after a tough round. Mallow is immaculately kept, as befits a championship course. The major hazards are the trees, which line the fairways, and the terrain, which is never level. You play downhill with the ball above your feet, uphill with the ball below your feet, and vice versa. You learn respect for the trees on the 1st hole (par 4) where a hook will send you under the skirts of the leylandii on the left-hand side of the left-sloping fairway. On the uphill 3rd (par 4) stay right of the big tree in the centre of the fairway. There are splendid views from the 4th tee (par 3) played downhill to a green that falls away towards the trees at the back. The 5th – a dogleg right – is particularly charming in late spring when the hawthorn all along the left side of the fairway is in bloom. The 7th is the trickiest hole on the outward nine. You drive up and over a hill (sloping to the right) to a fairway that bends to the right. Forget focusing on your stance for a moment and take in the terrific views over the course and countryside from the 8th green back up the hill. You can see the Ballyhoura Mountains to the north, with the long ridge of the Galtees further north and east. Musheramore Mountain is to the southwest. The 11th (par 3) and 12th (par 5) are in the middle of the course and feel more open. They are beautifully planted with flowering shrubs. Here you are more aware of other golfers on the course than on the tree-lined front nine. The 16th is a satisfying downhill pitch. Summon your energies for a par 5 uphill, followed by a long par 3 (180metres/197yards from the back tees) to finish. If you play well here you can play well anywhere. Mallow is a terrific test of golf.

DONERAILE
9 holes – par 68 (5720metres/5768yards)
Opposite Doneraile Forest Park on the R581.
Green Fees: IR£10 "Regardless".
Telephone: 022 24137

Doneraile is a short course. There is no par 5 and the longest par 4 is 392metres/429yards from the back tees. It's a delight to play because of the beauty and interest of the surroundings and the excellent condition of the course. The 1st tee is beside the finish of the world's first steeplechase in 1752 from the Protestant church in Buttevant (7km/4.5miles away) to Doneraile Church. (The riders could see the steeple as they galloped across fields, and jumped the hedges and ditches.) The 2nd tee box is to the left of the 1st fairway and you drive across the 1st fairway and in front of the green. (Your line is to the right of the green along the side of the hill.) But despite a couple of crossing holes, Doneraile doesn't feel tight. It is laid out over open parkland with mature trees, and is crossed by a valley and small river (Breigogue) that comes into play on the 6th/15th and 8th/17th holes. The 6th is a dogleg to the right. Men drive across the valley to the fairway (the ladies' tee is on the other side of the valley) which turns right alongside a graveyard. Big hitters will be tempted to go straight for the green. You have priority for your second shot. You then stand by the graveyard wall (reflecting on the dangers of being hit by a golf ball) while players tee off from the 7th. The rough and woodland along the right-hand boundary of the 7th falls steeply to the river. Then it's a par 3 back across the valley to a plateau green, backed by trees. The 9th/18th is the longest hole at Doneraile, played back up to the clubhouse. The greens (bent and fine fescues) are excellent and the club is gradually removing the leylandii on the course and replacing them with native hardwood trees. This can only enhance its charm.

FERMOY
18 holes – par 70
Signposted from the N8 about 3km/2miles south of the town.
Green Fees: IR£20 weekdays, IR£25 weekends and bank holidays.
Telephone: 025 32694

The club is friendly, the course open and honest, and the views splendid. It's a real pleasure to play Fermoy. The course lies on the slopes of Corrin Hill, a landmark for miles around, surmounted by a tall Celtic cross. Slopes is the operative word; there are not too many level lies at Fermoy. But the fairways are, mostly, generous and the course is lightly bunkered. It was laid out in the 1960s by Commander John Harris and is a course of two halves. The first nine zigzag down the hillside and up again. The back nine starts with the 10th (par 4) heading straight down the hill, followed by a steady progression back up. It's good exercise, but not exhausting. Between the front and back nines, separated by a short walk, there's a small road, little used except by the golf club. The only noise up here is birdsong. The view from the 1st tee is to the hilltop and the high stone cross on the hill. To your right, a huge vista over southeast Cork – fertile farmland and low hills rolls towards the distant horizon. By the 3rd (par 4) you'll realise that gravity has little sympathy for golfers. The side slopes are an excellent test of your shot-making skills. The splendid 6th has a blind second shot. As what you can see falls away steeply, you'll be tempted to overcompensate. Don't. You'll be astonished to find a relatively flat surface over the ridge. After the exhilarating, downhill 10th you'll appreciate the gorse- and tree-lined par 3 at the bottom of the hill. Then you climb up to the toughest hole on the course – the 13th (par 4). You drive steeply downhill, but the fairway undulates violently, veering both right and left. As you gaze up the 14th you'll be surprised to see it's stroke index 17. A long drive is needed to the dogleg left, from where your second shot is over a wide gully. Fermoy has little need of bunkers. Two have been added to the opening hole, but for aesthetic as much as technical reasons. There are hazards enough in the lie of the land, the trees, heather and gorse. The greens are hard and fast in summer. You'll be well tested at Fermoy.

Fota Island Golf Course

WATER ROCK
18 holes – par 70 (5664metres/6220yards)
Signposted from the N25 near Midleton.
Green Fees: IR£15 weekdays, IR£18 weekends and bank holidays.
Telephone: 021 613499

Water Rock's owners, the Healey family, have put a lot into Water Rock – a young pay and play course that has already established a reputation. A Patrick Merrigan design (Tulfarris, Woodenbridge, Faithlegg) is always intelligent, requiring a strategy for every hole. He has been no less exacting at Water Rock the wide fairways offering the only concession to the occasional golfer. The clubhouse sits on a hill with wonderful views of rolling farmland and most of the course, which falls away on three sides of the hill. There's a lot of new planting, but the trees are already well enough established to be a real hazard. The hillside has been incorporated into the design of the course, so you will encounter holes that play round the contours (the 2nd – par 5) downhill (the 3rd – par 3) and uphill to cleverly defended greens (the 18th – par 4). The 10th (par 5) leads you down from the clubhouse towards the Owenacurra River and several water features. The 11th (par 4) curves gently around a lake, with a pretty ladies' tee under some trees with its own pond. As you approach the green you may see a gaggle of people waiting by the 12th (par 3). On busy days, queues can form at par 3s, but this group will be here with a special purpose. The 12th is a magnificent hole played across a long lake, willows brushing the water on the right, trees lining the bank on the left, to a slightly raised green. From the back tees (there are three for the men to choose from) the carry is all of 183metres/200yards, yet the queue will be for the blue tees. Nearly every man and boy will stride to the blue tees, roll his shoulders like a pro and duff his drive into the lake. At the far end of the lake, feigning complete lack of interest, lies a swan on a magnificent nest raised above the rushes. Inevitably, this hole is called "Swan Lake". There is no better entertainment for miles around. The 13th (par 5) – cunningly bunkered and with a green on three levels – is no anti-climax. Two more holes are played around a lake, until a queue forms again – hope undiminished – to repeat the earlier "Swan Lake" performance across another lake at the 17th (par 3 and 197metres/216yards from the back tees) with a bunker in front of the green. Water Rock is a serious course that manages to be great fun too. The club is cheerful and unpretentious, the atmosphere friendly.

BEYOND THE 18TH GREEN

> *"'Tis the bells of Shandon*
> *That sound so grand on*
> *The pleasant waters of the River Lee"*

The city of **Cork** (Corcaigh – "Swamp" was founded by Saint Finbarr in the sixth or early seventh century on the banks of the River Lee. As its name suggests, it was a watery site. In fact the centre of the city is an island in the river, and in the eighteenth century, ocean-going ships docked in the deep waters over which Grand Parade and St Patrick's Street are built. Ships still dock at the quays in the heart of the city. Because of its turbulent history, most of the city buildings date from the nineteenth century. To the north of the river, the city climbs so steeply that the streets are like staircases. The skyline is all spires and steeples. **Saint Anne's Church** in Shandon was built in the eighteenth century on the site of a mediaeval church, which was destroyed by the Cromwellians. You can climb the tower and ring the eight **Bells of Shandon**, one of which bears the inscription

> *"We were all cast at Gloucester, in England."*

No visit to **Cork** would be complete without a visit to **Blarney Castle** and the famous **Blarney Stone**. Tradition says its sixteenth-century owner, Cormac MacCarthy, used his eloquence to avoid accepting the authority of Queen Elizabeth I of England. She said, "Blarney, what he says he does not mean. It's the usual Blarney". Which is why kissing the Blarney Stone is said to bestow the "gift of the gab". **Blarney Castle** (more accurately described as a fortified tower house) is not simply a tourist trap. It is one of the largest, best-preserved castles in Ireland and has lovely, landscaped gardens. It was built in the fifteenth century and was the strongest castle in the province of Munster. The walls are 5.5metres/18ft thick. The staircase is deliberately narrow so a single swordsman could defend it. The battlements on the square tower are 25metres/83ft above the ground. Above the entrance is the **Murder Hole** – a machicolation (removable stone or space between corbels for dropping missiles or boiling oil on attackers). The Blarney Stone is actually one of the machicolations on a parapet on the roof of the castle. To kiss it, you must lie on your back and hold on tightly to iron supports while you drop your head backwards over the gap through which the boiling oil would have been poured.

Cobh (An Cóbh – "The Cove") on **Great Island** (signposted from the N25) is a lovely, lively seaside town. Terraces of brightly painted houses lead up from the water's edge to the striking Victorian Gothic style **St Colman's Cathedral** (built between 1868 and 1915), which commands a view of **Cork Harbour** and the sea beyond. The cathedral bells ring out at three-hour intervals between 9am and 6pm. They were heard by some of the two and a half million emigrants who sailed from here. These are commemorated by a bronze sculpture beside the converted Victorian Railway Station, which houses **The Queenstown Story** – the history of the port, and the emigrants who left from it. (**Cobh** was named Queenstown after a visit by Queen Victoria in 1849.) The sculpture depicts **Annie Moore** and **Anthony Phillip**, the first emigrants to pass through the Ellis Island Immigration Centre off New York in 1892. (Annie Moore was the first to step on the island and was given a $10 gold piece.) **Cobh** was the last port of call of the Titanic in 1912. Victims of the Lusitania, torpedoed in 1915, are commemorated in a memorial on the quay. They are buried in Clonmel Churchyard 2km/1.25miles outside the town. It is also the burial place of **Charles Wolfe** who wrote the much-anthologised poem *The Burial of Sir John Moore after Corunna*.

The **Fota Estate** on **Fota Island** has, besides the golf course, a **Wildlife Park** and an **Arboretum**. The free-ranging residents of the **Wildlife Park** include giraffes, ostriches, antelopes, kangaroos, wallabies, and lemurs. The park specialises in breeding endangered species in captivity. It is the world's leading breeder of cheetahs – one of the few animals in the park that can only be viewed through a fence. There are pools for flamingos and penguins. (Open Monday–Saturday 17th March to 30th September 10am–6pm, Sundays 11am–5pm. Open weekends January, February, early March and October. Telephone: 021 812678) The **Arboretum** surrounds **Fota House**, built as a shooting lodge and enlarged and redesigned by Richard Morrison in the Regency period. The trees and shrubs are clearly labelled with their country of origin and date of planting. The great sequoia was planted in 1847 – only two years after the first plantings in England. (**Arboretum** always accessible.) The clubhouse of **Fota Island Golf Club** is the former stable block of **Fota House**.

Nearby **Barryscourt Castle** (Caisleann Chuirt an Bharraigh) was established by the Anglo-Norman de Barry family who acquired the land in the twelfth century. It is another excellent and well-preserved example of a fifteenth-century fortified tower house. It is a square keep within a bawn (enclosing outer wall) with three corner towers intact. The ground floor houses an exhibition on the history of the castle and the de Barry family.

You can learn about the difference between **Irish Whiskey** and Scotch at the **Jameson Heritage Centre** in **Midleton**. There were once 400 tiny distilleries making whiskey in Ireland. Now, all the well-known Irish whiskeys (except Bushmills) are distilled in **Midleton**. Daily guided-tours of the old distillery take you through the whole process from harvesting the barley to maturing in special barrels before bottling. Don't be afraid to raise your hand if the guide asks for volunteers at the end of the tour. You will be volunteering to taste some whiskeys. (Telephone: 021 613594)

The R626 from **Midleton** to **Fermoy** follows the **Owenacurra River** (Abhainn na Cora – "River of the Weir") up a steep-sided, narrow, wooded valley. North of the valley the R626 joins the N8 from Cork. Turn right for a short (8km/5miles) detour to **Castlelyons**, which has a ruined fourteenth-century friary and church and the ivy-clad shell of a fifteenth-century castle all built by the de Barry family.

You can see **Corrin Cross**, high on a hill above **Fermoy** (Mainistir Fhear Maighe – "Monastery of the Men of the Plain"). Fermoy was a garrison town in the eighteenth and nineteenth centuries but is now best known as a centre for salmon fishing in the **Blackwater** (Abhainn Mór – "Great River").

The romantic, wild garden at **Anne's Grove** in the verdant valley of the **Awbeg River** (Abha Bheag – "Little River") is midway between **Fermoy** and **Mallow** and **Fermoy** and **Doneraile**. It is signposted in the picturesque village of **Castletownroche** (Baile Chaisleáin an Róistigh – "Town of Roche's Castle") on the river. The sloping grounds surrounding the eighteenth-century house are divided into three garden areas – the riverside, the glen and the walled garden – planted in the naturalised style made popular in the nineteenth century by William Robinson, author of The Wild Garden (1870). Rhododendrons and azaleas line the woodland walk. A water garden, with rustic bridges and a lily pond, is laid out along a small tributary river. (Open 10am–5pm Monday to Friday, 1pm–6pm Saturday and Sunday. Telephone: 022 26145)

Doneraile and **Buttevant** are on the **Awbeg** further upriver. **Doneraile** (Dún Air Aill – "Fort on the Cliff") once formed part of the estate granted to the poet **Edmund Spenser**, author of *The Faerie Queen*. He lived and worked as an English administrator at nearby **Kilcolman Castle** (Cill Cholmáin – "Colman's Church") between 1587 and 1598. His scorched earth policy and near genocidal

views of the Irish were regarded as extreme, even by his fellow administrators. The castle was attacked and burned by the Irish in 1598. **Spenser** returned to England. **Kilcolman Castle** is a sad ruin in a field. Little remains of the castle. Spenser's son sold **Doneraile** to the St Leger family in 1627.

The name **Buttevant** is derived either from the Norman French word botavant meaning a defensive earthwork, or the de Barry war cry "Boutez en Avant". A ruined de Barry castle stands on a rock overhanging the river. The ruins of a thirteenth-century Franciscan monastery also overlook the river. The world's first steeplechase, in 1752, was from the Protestant church in **Buttevant** to the Protestant church in **Doneraile** – its steeple clearly visible 7km/4.5miles away. (The church is beside the first tee at **Doneraile Golf Course**.) The **St Leger** family grave is in the churchyard. (The St Leger Stakes, run at Doncaster, is the world's oldest classic horse race). The **St Leger** family built **Doneraile Court** in 1730. It is surrounded by 166hectares/412acres of landscaped gardens and oak woods. The demesne is now a public park with a herd of red deer. The restored house is also open to the public. (Park open mid-April to October, weekdays 8am–8.30pm, weekends and bank holidays 11am–7pm; November to mid-April, weekdays 8am–4.30pm, weekends and bank holidays 10am–4.30pm. Telephone: 022 24244)

> *"Beauing, belleing, dancing, drinking*
> *Breaking windows, damning, singing,*
> *Ever raking, never thinking,*
> *Live the rakes of Mallow."*

Mallow (Machaire Rátha – "Plain of the Ringfort") is the largest town in the **Blackwater Valley**. In the eighteenth and nineteenth centuries it was a spa town, featured in the well-known song "The Rakes of Mallow". Today it is a busy market town. From here the N20 takes you back to **Cork** and **Blarney Castle**.

TOURIST INFORMATION

Cork/Kerry Tourism: Tourist House, Grand Parade, Cork. Telephone: 021 273251

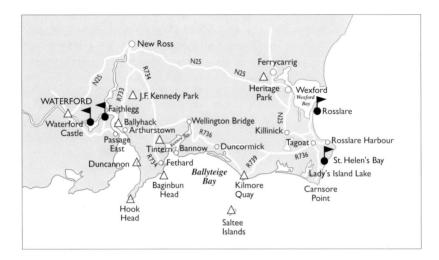

(Golf Courses: Rosslare, St Helen's Bay, Waterford Castle and Faithlegg.)

Distances: Wexford to Rosslare 21km/13miles; Rosslare to Waterford (via Passage East) 48km/30miles; Waterford to New Ross 27km/17miles; New Ross to Wexford 31km/19miles.

The southeast corner of Ireland is one of the most historic areas of the country. Traces of Bronze Age kitchens, where deer was cooked, have been found along the coast. The Celts, early Christians, Vikings, Normans and Elizabethans have all left their stamp on the landscape. The Vikings named Wexford and Waterford. The Anglo-Normans landed near Rosslare in the twelfth century. They intermarried with the great Irish families, founded abbeys, built castles and became more Irish than the Irish. Their legacy is visible in the fourteenth century tower houses that dot the landscape, and in the Old English townland names. Golfers will find this the sunniest and driest corner of Ireland.

ROSSLARE
18 holes – par 72 (6031metres/6601yards)
12 holes – par 46 (3615metres/3956yards)

Green Fees: IR£25 weekdays, IR£35 weekends (18 holes);
IR£11 (12 holes); IR£17 (24 holes).
Telephone: 053 32113

Rosslare is a long-established (1905) well-bunkered links, laid out on a long, narrow peninsula separating Wexford harbour from the Irish Sea and Rosslare Bay. The holes run out along the sea and back in a figure of eight shape. It is not an easy course, but the lovely turf, excellent greens and interesting views of the sea and Rosslare harbour make it always a pleasure to play. It is particularly nice in spring and summer when the rough is filled with low-growing, creamy burnet roses. Your first drive is through a short avenue of trees to a fairway that doglegs left with a mound and two big bunkers to stop you cutting the corner. If the course is busy the start can be slow, because this short par 4 (340metres/372yards from the blue tees) is followed by a par 3. But then you get into your stride on a tough par 5 with deadly rough and a boomerang-shaped fairway. The 4th (par 4) takes you over a ridge on the narrow fairway, towards the sea and a view of Rosslare harbour and the cross-Channel ferries. The 5th is a long par 4 that doglegs left. Bunkers guard the crook. Two bunkers and a depression in the fairway about 55metres/60yards from the green make the approach very tricky. Men have a long carry to the narrow, twisting fairway that narrows dramatically again before the sunken green on the 7th (par 5). The 11th is a long, difficult dogleg right (par 4) with a blind approach over a marker on a mound to the green. There's a fine sequence of par 4s along the sea (on your left) and usually into the wind before you turn to get the wind behind you for the par 5 finish to a green nicely framed in the trees that surround the clubhouse.

Rosslare's second layout begins behind the 8th tee on the original links. (The entrance is a mile further along the road.) Twelve holes are laid out over this flatter ground on the Wexford harbour side of the peninsula. But there is water, in the shape of a deep channel and pond, to add interest at the beginning of your round. And there are fine views across the harbour to Wexford and the Blackstairs Mountains beyond.

ST HELEN'S BAY GOLF & COUNTRY CLUB
18 holes – par 72 (6091metres/6667yards)
Signposted from the N25 at Kilrane, near Rosslare harbour.
Green Fees: May to September IR£22 weekdays IR£25 weekends and bank holidays; October to April IR£18 weekdays, IR£20 weekends and bank holidays.
Telephone: 053 33234

The course is laid out in an L shape over 150 acres of parkland which gently sweep up to a headland overlooking St Helen's Bay. The design, by Philip Walton, put water into play on nine holes, incorporated a restored "famine wall"(part of a nineteenth-century "work for welfare" scheme) and planted 5,000 trees. When these mature, this course will be even more of a challenge. Water is most dangerous on a sequence of strong holes from the 9th to the 12th – the latter a long par 4 (stroke index 1) where a stream (out-of-bounds) runs along the left-hand side of the narrow fairway and crosses, just where the fairway broadens, in front of the green. You are now at the corner of the L and the section of the course, which runs up to the headland. You are working your way towards two terrific finishing holes. On the 14th you get your first glimpse of the sea from the elevated green. The 15th is a long par 4. The wind may be against you, compounding your difficulties. There is a lovely view of the bay from the 16th tee and the parkland has become a links. You can taste the salt air as you walk from the 16th green to the 17th tee. What you now see before you is a card-wrecking par 3. To your left is out-of-bounds – the cliff and the strand below. The green is tucked into mounds, the narrow entrance guarded by a bunker. The 18th is a short, but narrow, par 4. There is a wall and a palm tree on the right, with the cliff and strand again to your left. You drive over mounds, right in your line of flight. A truly memorable conclusion.

WATERFORD CASTLE
18 holes – par 72 (6231metres/6819yards)
3km/2miles from Waterford on the R683
(fourth turn left after Regional Hospital roundabout)
6km/4miles from Passage East ferry on R683.
Green Fees: IR£27 Monday to Thursday, IR£30 Friday to Sunday
and bank holidays. Telephone: 051 871633

There are half a dozen island courses in Ireland, but they are nearly all joined to the mainland by causeways. Waterford Castle is the exception. You drive on to an old-fashioned chain-driven ferry to get to the course, on Little Island in the middle of the wide and peaceful estuary of the River Suir. You can see the castle, (now a hotel attached to the golf course), through a gap in the trees to your right near the 1st green. There's room for 36 holes on the parkland surrounding the castle, so there is a consequent sense of space. The fairways are generous, if well bunkered. But if you keep straight, you might even play to your handicap here, as well as enjoying the splendid river views. The course architects (Des Smyth and Declan Brannigan) have planted new trees to add to the mature stands of trees on the estate, and introduced five artificial lakes. The first of these comes into play at the 2nd (par 3) where you drive over the edge of the lake to the green. Water is more dangerously in play on the 3rd and 4th (both par 4). (As you tee off on the 4th you may see the incongruous sight of a large ship hoving into view ahead in the estuary.) Big hitters might be able to cut the corner on the 5th (par 5) – but only until the newly planted trees mature. The 12th is a tricky par 4. The bunkers, where the narrowing fairway bends to the right, make you think carefully about where to place your drive. The nicest view of the river is from the

13th (a par 5, dogleg right with bunkers and out-of-bounds all along the right-hand side of the fairway). On the 16th you could be looking at the stern of a cargo ship docking in the estuary. The closing holes take you away from the river and back up the slope towards the clubhouse.

FAITHLEGG

18 holes – par 72 (6098metres/6674yards)
Signposted from the R683, 6km/4 miles from Waterford,
8km/5miles from Passage East.
Green Fees: IR£22 Monday to Thursday, IR£27 Fridays, weekends
and bank holidays, IR£16 before 9am Monday to Thursday.
(Reduced green fees for hotel guests.)
Telephone: 051 382241

You can always expect a good design from Patrick Merrigan. Faithlegg is no exception. The course is built in the grounds of Faithlegg House, an old estate, now a hotel. It lies between a low, wooded hill and the banks of the River Suir. The first three holes, and the 17th and 18th lie to the front of the formal, neoclassical building. The most obvious feature on these holes is water, in the shape of five ponds. But the most striking feature of the course as a whole is the way mature trees on the estate have been incorporated into the design. Three fine Spanish oaks along the left side of the 1st fairway make an otherwise straightforward opening more interesting. A long-hitter could almost drive the green. Those who hook the opening drive under the spreading branches will lose the chance of beginning the round with a par or a birdie. The 2nd runs along the boundary of the course. You will see from the rushy fields on the other side of the fence that this is not land made for golf. The lush fairways of Faithlegg have been created by basing the entire course on sand. Laurels, rhododendron and trees encircle the 4th green. You walk through the shrubbery to the 5th and your first sight of the wide and winding river. The 5th to 16th holes are bounded by the old estate walls, the river, and a tributary stream. A majestic native oak tree on the 8th calls for careful consideration placing your drive. Although it looks as though the fairway curves left, it is actually a dogleg right to a green down by the river. Your line on the uphill 13th (par 5) is the silver birch silhouetted against the sky at the top of the hill. (You can see Waterford Castle golf course across the river on your right.) The lovely 16th (par 3) is completely surrounded by trees and shrubs. A revetted bunker has been added at the back of the green. Golfers who were straight but too long were unduly penalised by the shrubbery. Now you have a chance of saving par with a decent bunker shot. Then it's through the shrubbery to the closing holes in the parkland in front of the house. The 17th is a dogleg right beside the rhododendron-lined avenue. Three lovely, spreading oaks and a pond on the left make this long par 4 (397metres/435yards) a real challenge.

A walk through Wexford is a walk through Irish history. The Vikings called it Waesfjord – sea-washed. They raided the rest of Ireland from here, and built up the port. Names like Keyser Lane and Selskar, and the name of the town itself, are reminders of the Viking past. **Selskar Abbey** (built by the Normans) near **West Gate** is thought to stand on an earlier site of worship of the Norse God, Odin. The Normans came in 1170. They fortified the town and laid out the narrow streets, winding down to the **River Slaney** (Sléine). The only trace of the fortifications is the **West Gate Tower** housing the **Heritage Centre**. The **Bull Ring**, the small square in the centre of the town, is a reminder of the bull-baiting that was popular in mediaeval times. This is where Cromwell killed two thousand townspeople of **Wexford** after the town refused to surrender. A sculpture of an Irish pikeman commemorates the Wexfordmen killed in the 1798 Rebellion. On **The Crescent** by the harbour there is a bronze statue of **Commodore John Barry**, the founder of the US Navy, who emigrated from Wexford in the eighteenth century.

The **Irish National Heritage Park** (signposted on the N11 and N25) has been imaginatively created on the site of one of the first Norman strongholds in Ireland. The lime-washed castle is a replica of a Norman feudal manor. Other full-scale models reconstruct the homes, tombs and places of worship – pagan and Christian – of Ireland's earliest inhabitants. The Viking ship is modelled on a longboat (found in Denmark) built in Ireland around AD1060. On some bank holidays and when special events are staged, meat is cooked in a Bronze Age **Fulacht Fiadh** (deer cooking pit). These have been found along the coast and beside rivers. The meat was wrapped in straw and cooked in a pit of water heated with hot stones from a fire. (When the stones cooled, they cracked. **Fulachta Fiadha** are identified by U-shaped mounds of cracked burned stones by a water source.) The meat takes much the same time to cook as it does in a conventional oven – twenty minutes per half kilo (1lb) and twenty over. (Open daily 9.30am–6.30pm. Telephone: 053 20733)

Rosslare (Ros Láir – "Middle Headland") is famous for its 10km/6mile-strand, which has the coveted EC Blue Flag guarantee of cleanliness. **Kelly's Resort Hotel** on the strand has a terrific permanent collection of Irish art. There are often special exhibitions as well. (Telephone: 053 32114)

Lady's Island Lake, a land-locked sea lagoon, (signposted from the R736), has one of the largest breeding colonies of terns in Ireland, including the rare roseate tern. On **Our Lady's Island** are the ruins of an Augustinian priory dedicated to the Blessed Virgin and the remains of a thirteenth-century Norman castle. It is still a place of pilgrimage.

From the fishing port of **Kilmore Quay** (Cill Mhór – "Big Church") with its picturesque harbour, brightly painted fishing fleet and thatched cottages you can go sea-fishing or take a boat trip around the **Saltee Islands**, 6km/4miles offshore. The uninhabited islands are home to enormous colonies of puffins, kittiwakes, guillemots, razorbills and gulls. (Telephone: 051 29684 Saltee Island Cruises/053 29704 Kilmore Quay Boat Charter)

The lost town of **Bannow** (Cuan an Bhainbh – "Harbour of the Suckling Pig") on **Bannow Bay** was established by the Normans after their landing at **Baginbun Head** on the other side of the bay in May 1169. The town and port they established was buried when the bay silted up. By the end of the eighteenth century it had all but vanished. All that remains is the ruined thirteenth-century **St Mary's Church**.

Tintern Abbey, also known as **Tintern de Voto** ("of the Vow") stands by a stream flowing into **Bannow Bay**. It was founded in 1200 by William, Earl Marshal of Pembroke, as the result of a promise made during a terrible storm at sea. It is named for the Cistercian abbey at Tintern in the Wye Valley, in England. Like many other great abbeys, it was built over and became a residence after the dissolution of the monasteries by Henry VIII in 1540. The abbey has been restored by Dúchas (The Heritage Service). There are many lovely pathways in the wooded grounds of the abbey estate. You can walk along a riverside path to **Saltmills** on **Bannow Bay**. (Grounds always open, abbey open May to October 9.30am–6.30pm. Telephone: 051 562650)

The road from here to the rocky shore at **Hook Head** passes the lovely beach at **Fethard** (Fiodh Ard – "High Wood"). Henry II gave the **Hook** to the Knights Templars. Raymond de Gros built the distinctive black and white painted **Lighthouse** in the twelfth century. (Lighthouse open daily March to October 9.30am–5.30 pm, guided tours. Telephone: 051 397055/054) The well-known saying "by hook or by crook" is said to refer to Cromwell's determination to take the town of **Waterford** by **Hook** or by **Crooke** – a village on the other side of **Waterford Harbour**. It's also supposed to have been said by sailors approaching the deep, natural harbour on the **River Suir**.

Duncannon Fort (Dún Canann – "Canainn's Fort") on a promontory west of the village, has been occupied by every military power that passed through the area from the Stone Age to the modern Irish Army. An early Irish chieftain gave the fort its name. The Normans strengthened it. The Elizabethans reinforced it again as a defence against the Armada. The Cromwellians captured it from the Irish troops loyal to Charles I. James II sailed from it after his defeat by William of Orange at the Battle of the Boyne. Finally, the Irish Army used it as a training base. It is now open to the public. (Open daily June to mid-September, 10am–5.30pm. Telephone: 051 389454)

Tintern Abbey, Wexford

A car ferry from **Ballyhack** (Baile Shac – "Homestead of Dung") to Passage East on the opposite bank of the **River Suir** (Siúr – "Sister") is the short cut from here to **Waterford**. Henry II gave **Ballyhack** to the Knights Hospitallers who built the ruined castle that overlooks the estuary. (Castle open daily June to September, 10am–6pm. Telephone: 051 389468) The Norman invader, Richard de Clare, known as **Strongbow**, landed at **Passage East** (An Pasáiste – "The Passage") with twelve hundred knights in 1170 and marched to **Waterford**. (He arrived at the

behest of the King of Leinster, Dermot MacMurrough, who was at war with other chieftains. Strongbow married MacMurrough's daughter, and became MacMurrough's heir.)

Waterford is another historic port. The Vikings called it Vadrafjord. **Reginald's Tower**, 24metres/80ft tall, built in 1003, stands at the end of the wide stone quay that stretches along the south bank of the river. The inscription over the main entrance says it was built by Reginald the Norseman. (Open weekdays Easter to October 10am–5pm, weekends 2pm–6pm. Telephone: 051 873501)

Saint Olaf's Church, behind the tower, was an early Viking foundation (c870). The Normans rebuilt it when they conquered the city in 1170. The city was ravaged by the Cromwellians in 1649 and rebuilt substantially in the eighteenth and nineteenth centuries. The Church of Ireland neoclassical **Cathedral** (1770) was designed by a local architect, John Roberts, and is considered the finest eighteenth-century church in Ireland. (He also designed the Catholic **Cathedral** nearly 30 years later.) The Waterford Treasures Museum in **The Granary** on the quay has jewellery, artefacts and weapons, from the Viking and Norman past, excavated in the city. (Open June to August 9.30am–9pm, rest of the year 10am–5pm. Telephone: 051 304500)

A fine example of an antique **Waterford Crystal** chandelier hangs in **Waterford City Hall** – a Georgian building dating from 1788 – in **The Mall**. The industry was established in 1783 and the hand-blown, hand-cut crystal is famous worldwide. You can see glass blowing and cutting demonstrations during the popular tours of the factory, about 2km/1mile from the city centre. (Showroom and factory open daily, April to September 8.30am–6pm, last tour 4pm; November to March 9am–5pm, last tour 3.15pm. Telephone: 051 332500)

The R733 to **New Ross** takes you past some of the most beautiful ruins in Ireland. The large, well-preserved Cistercian ruins of twelfth-century **Dunbrody Abbey** (Dún Bróithe –"Brody's Fort") stand in a lovely setting near the river. There is a large, aisled nave, six transepts and a fifteenth-century tower.

The **John F Kennedy Park & Arboretum** (also signposted from the N25) was opened in 1968 to commemorate the assassinated president whose great-grandfather emigrated to the United States from nearby **Dunganstown** (Baile Uí Dhonnagáin – "Homestead of Donnagán"). From the top of Slieve Coillte (Coillte – "Woods") in the park you can see for miles. This vast park has about 5,000 trees and shrubs from all over the world. In the summer months you can take a tour of the park by pony and trap. (Open all year. Telephone: 051 388171)

The narrow, winding streets of **New Ross** (Rhos Mhic Thriúin – "Wood of Treon's Son") climbing steeply from the river, are a reminder of its mediaeval Norman foundation. The town is beautifully situated on the **River Barrow** just south of its meeting with the **River Nore** (An Fheoir). Only fragments of the Norman walls remain. The town was taken by the Cromwellians in 1649. It was later captured, lost again and burned in one of the last battles of the ill-fated and tragic 1798 Rebellion. You can take a two-hour cruise from the quay, up the beautiful, wide, quiet river. (Classic Galley Cruises, April to October. Tel: 051 421723)

TOURIST INFORMATION

Wexford Tourist Information Office: The Cresent Quay, Wexford
Telephone: 053 23111
Waterford Tourist Information Office: 41 The Quay, Waterford
Telephone: 051 875788
Dúchas (The Heritage Service): 51 St. Stephen's Green, Dublin 2
Telephone: 01 647 3000

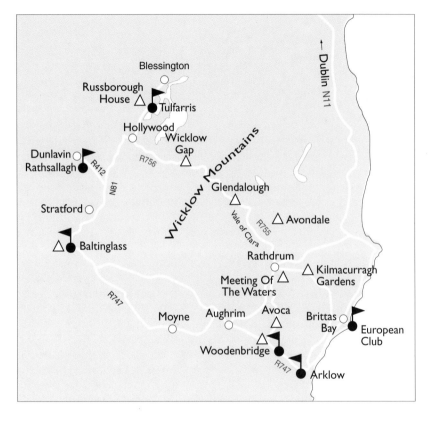

(Golf Courses: Tulfarris, Rathsallagh, Baltinglass, The European Club, Woodenbridge and Arklow)

Distances: Arklow to Glendalough 34km/21miles; Blessington to Baltinglass 30km/19miles; Blessington to Glendalough 33km/21miles; Brittas Bay to Arklow 27km/17miles.

The spine of the dark brown and purple Wicklow Mountains divides east and west Wicklow. In the west, rivers flow from mountain lakes through wide valleys to the plains of Kildare. In the east, rivers flow from deep, dark glens, down narrow, wooded valleys to the sea. Only one road cuts through the Wicklow Mountains from north to south – the "Military Road" that the British built to root out the Irish rebels in 1798. Wicklow has two names. In Irish it is Cill Mhantáin – The Church of Mantan, companion of Saint Patrick. The Vikings called it Wyking alo – Viking Meadow – hence, Wicklow. It is also called The Garden County.

TULFARRIS
18 holes – par 72 (6404metres/7116yards)
8km/5miles south of Blessington, signposted from N81.
Green Fees: IR£40 weekdays; IR£50 weekends and bank holidays
Telephone: 045 867644

When you play Tulfarris you reach for superlatives. The setting – a mature eighteenth-century estate along the shores of Poulaphouca Lake – is superb. The design (by Patrick Merrigan) is supremely intelligent. This you realize from the 1st hole (par 5) – a gentle dogleg left, skirting a pond. The bunkers reduce your options the closer you get to the green. The 2nd is a long par 3 over a pond into the prevailing westerly wind. The 3rd (par 4) is fiendishly bunkered all the way to the well-protected green. You get the message. Yet this is a fair course. It will test every aspect of your golf, rewarding accurate play and careful club selection. The latter is as important here as on a links course. The often-blustery wind whips around the lake. At the 7th (par 5) take a moment to stand on the championship tee. This calls for a drive across a corner of the lake through a gap in the trees. From the blue tees it's an awesome 556metres/608yards. For ordinary men it's 533 yards, for ladies it's a mere 426metres/466yards by comparison. Your second is a blind shot over a brow as the hole curves to the right with the shore. The fairway slopes left towards the water. The 10th (par 4) is a roller coaster with a fairway sloping violently left to impede your progress to the lakeside green. The wind is likely to be the biggest factor as you try to hit straight at the (par 3) 11th. Going back up the hill on the 12th (par 4), mature trees demand an accurately placed drive for a clear shot at the green. You'll make another two trips to the lake in the final six holes, and finish in a blaze of glory. (The magnificent Palladian mansion you can see across the lake is Russborough House, one of the finest Georgian houses in Ireland.) The 17th (par 4) is idiosyncratic – a sharp dogleg left over a pond, and virtually a blind drive towards the bunker that seems to lie across the entire fairway at driving distance, but which actually marks the right-hand edge of the fairway. At the 18th (par 4) you drive over water. There's a lot of sand to catch a slice. The sloping green is almost entirely protected at the front by a large pond. Will you make a final, heroic assault on the centre of the green, or lay up on the increasingly narrow approach? Tulfarris is always asking you questions. The course manager, Adrian Williams has attracted prestige events. But don't be put off by the length from the back tees. There's a choice of 4 tees for men, reducing the length to a manageable 5719metres/6260yards from the front tees and ladies play it at 5213metres/5705yards. The great achievement of this course is that every category is challenged, and treated fairly. You must take your hat off to Tulfarris. The water-features that have been added don't seem intrusive or unnatural. The overall feeling is of a design that works with the natural features of the landscape. You will feel like a million dollars if you play it well.

RATHSALLAGH
18 holes – par 72 (6319metres/6916yards)
Signposted from the N81 about 19km/12miles from Blessington.
Green Fees: IR£40 Monday to Thursday, IR£50 Friday to Sunday
and bank holidays.
Breakfast special: before 10am (including breakfast at Rathsallagh House)
IR£45 April to October, IR£35 November to March.
Telephone: 045 403316

It takes about 100 acres to lay out a golf course comfortably. Some occupy less space. Not so Rathsallagh which is set in 252 acres of beautiful parkland around Rathsallagh House, the well known country house hotel. While the two are connected, the golf course is not a mere adjunct to the hotel. It has its own clubhouse and entrance, accessed from the road, and feels like a club with an independent life and membership. Indeed the hotel is only visible from a small part of the course, which sweeps through mature woodland, across lakes and streams, and across and around the large valley which divides the two buildings. The course, designed by Peter McEvoy and Christy O'Connor Jnr, is scenic and full of interest. The 1st – a par 5, with the fairway sloping towards out-of-bounds on the left, and a well defended green – is not an easy start. Water comes into play on the 4th (par 3) – more of it than you can see from the tee, so be careful. The 6th has a complicated network of streams and ponds down its length, which may have you wading for your ball. Your entire strategy on the 8th (par 4) will be governed by first avoiding, then crossing an erratic body of water to a well-defended green. A long pull up the hill to the clubhouse completes a tough front nine. The (par 4) 10th (par 5 for ladies) sets off down the hill again towards a very pretty water feature with a waterfall. Only a shot of great authority will see you onto the green in two, rather than hunting in the plantation to the left of the green, or in the lake in front of it. But from here the character of the course changes, heading off into the country for three holes with no water at all. If you've been discouraged by your score on the front nine, you now have a chance to regain your confidence as the course works its way round the side of the valley to the 15th (par 4). The 16th (par 5) heads down into the valley again to a particularly pretty corner but, in case you have become over confident, the long par 3 at the 17th (154metres/169yards) requires an accurate shot to avoid one of several bunkers. The 18th – a long par 4 – is a reminder of how tough the earlier holes have been. You have a difficult second shot to a tiered green. Even if you make it in two, you'll need to putt like a pro to make par.

BALTINGLASS
9 holes – par 68 (5554metres/6171yards)
Baltinglass village.
Green Fees: IR£10 weekdays, IR£12 weekends and bank holidays.
Telephone: 0508 81350

Baltinglass golf club sits above the village in part of a former estate planted with oak, chestnut, maple and beech, around which the course is laid out. In the centre of it all is the clubhouse, from whose long conservatory there are extensive views over the course and the 9th/18th green. The 1st (par 4) straight uphill, with a stream to catch your drive, feels very long, and there's a tricky tiered green with hidden bunkers at the back to catch hefty approach shots. The 2nd (par 4) rewards you with a magnificent view from the tee of the village and the ruined abbey. Stop and listen to the wind swishing through the fir plantation behind you, like the sound of running water. There's a gigantic sweep down this right-hand dogleg through an avenue of trees (oak, beech, maple and chestnut) to the green beside the clubhouse. The 3rd is a tricky par 3 played over a large field maple. From here you set off into the flatter country on three long par 4s. A spreading chestnut narrows the approach to the 6th, after which you'll be glad to play the 7th (par 3) with bunkers to the front and a treacherous bank at the back – and trees of course. Two shorter par 4s complete a delightful 9 holes. The front nine is just 2809metres/3074yards, but the long par 4s (there's no par 5 for men) and the steep hill on the first make it feel longer. The second time around, different tee positions make it a mite shorter (2745metres/3004yards). Baltinglass is lovingly tended by the head greenkeeper, Martin Donegan. The first green is sand-based; the rest are soil-based with meadow grasses. They are all beautifully maintained. Don't worry if there is no one around to take your green fee. Put it in the honesty box and enjoy the tranquillity of the course. The club has applied for planning permission to lay out a second nine holes at the top of the hill.

THE EUROPEAN CLUB
18 holes – par 71 (6113metres/6690yards)
On the R750. Signposted from the N11 at Brittas Bay.
Green Fees: IR£140 for a 4-round ticket (valid one year).
IR£60 April–October, IR£45 November–March.
Telephone: 0404 47415

In the 1930s, Bobby Jones, one of the finest golfers the world has ever seen, built a golf course on his own land at Augusta, Georgia. The great golf architect Alister Mackenzie designed it. Bobby Jones invited the best golfers of his generation to play it. It's a tradition continued in the US Masters tournament at Augusta every year. Pat Ruddy is an amateur golfer in the true sense of loving the game. He lives and breathes golf. As writer, editor, tournament organiser, developer and course designer he has made his living from it. In 1986, he mortgaged himself to the hilt, got an EC grant and bought land at Brittas Bay on the Wicklow coast. Then he designed and built a golf links on it. The European Club is now, like Augusta, listed among the top golf courses in the world. It runs through sand-hills above and along Brittas Bay. The fairways undulate towards greens, which sit snugly in the dunes and seem to follow the natural contours of the land. The native grasses on the dunes, greens and fairways enhance the naturalness. Here and there are clumps of gorse. Tall, graceful reeds line the marshlands and the stream, which are natural hazards on the 7th – a splendid hole. The only apparent improvements to nature are the railway sleepers on steep-backed bunkers and the audacious water hazard on the 18th. You will have difficulty choosing your favourite hole. Pat Ruddy particularly likes the 10th. It characteristically invites you to drive past bunkers to a generous landing area, then offers a narrow funnel-like approach to the green tucked into sheltering dunes. The 17th offers ladies the best of the tee positions with an exhilarating downhill drive to a sheltered fairway before another tantalisingly narrow uphill approach to the green nestling in the dunes. Several holes run along the sea. "The beach is in play. Play it as it lies. You may ground the club." (Local rule.) Bobby Jones was a millionaire in the days when the word meant wealth beyond most imaginings. He could afford to invite the best golfers of his generation to play at Augusta as his guests. Playing at Augusta is still a privilege afforded only to the very best and the very rich. Pat Ruddy built the European Club for lovers of golf. It's open to all who can afford

Woodenbridge Golf Course

Arklow Golf Course

the relatively modest green fees. The best compliment you can pay him is to play your best on it.

WOODENBRIDGE

18 holes – par 71 (5709metres/6344yards)
8km/5miles north of Arklow on the Rathdrum road.
Green Fees: IR£27 weekdays, IR£35 weekends and bank holidays.
Telephone: 0402 35202

> *"Billiard grass, bunkers*
> *Like golden bathtubs,*
> *Desmesne trees under which*
> *The ball flew like a pheasant."*

(Poem by James Liddy 1941 in Woodenbridge clubhouse.)

Pheasants feature at Woodenbridge. A pretty, thatched hut, with a fox and pheasant in thatch on the roof, stands by the entrance. But your first view of the course is likely to be from above, as you approach from the Wicklow Gap. After the wildness of the mountain, it is a surprise to see the beautiful parkland stretching along a curve of a broad river. On closer inspection you see that there are two rivers, the Avoca and the Aughrim, which meet beside the 11th green. Woodenbridge is another Patrick Merrigan design and he has not fought with nature: the water is entirely natural – merely diverted here and there. The bunkering of course, is pure Merrigan. The members have indulged themselves a little as well. At the 13th you'll find another delightful thatched construction surrounded by gorse and sporting a pheasant on the roof. It is that most rare of golfing creature comforts, the flushing lavatory. Another pretty thatched hut (no amenities) gives shelter near the 10th tee. If the 1st (par 4) lulls you into thinking this is a gentle course, you will change your mind as you face into the wind on the 2nd (par 4). The narrow valley, in which the course lies, is a funnel for the wind straight off the mountain. You see how well the course design uses the space available. Nowhere is there a sense of crowding, yet the boundaries – rivers on one side and steeply wooded hills on the other – are factors on eleven holes. The vegetation is mixed, with a number of tall pines, but also dogwood, young native hardwoods and a great bank of gorse between the 13th and 15th holes. And don't be surprised to see real pheasants at this end of the course. You'll not be troubled by the water until the 8th (par 3) where you play over an island to the green. You cross the river on a pretty twin-arched bridge. (Don't try to retrieve balls from the fast flowing river.) The 9th (par 5) is a monster calling for a drive over a lake, with trees and the Avoca River all down the right-hand side. You'll be glad to turn your back to the wind for five holes, which may flatter your score, but prepare for a tough finish over the closing four holes, two of them par 5s. The 17th (par 3) calls for total accuracy over water to a sloping green. The 18th (par 5) needs a drive of nearly 183metres/200yards upstream, just to make the fairway. This is a deeply satisfying course that you'll want to play again and again. If you could play all your golf here and at Arklow, a completely natural links, you would have little need to travel anywhere else.

ARKLOW
18 holes – par 68 (5434metres/5947yards)
South of the town centre in Arklow (signposted).
Green Fees: IR£20.
Telephone: 0402 32971/32492

Arklow members describe their course as "an 18 hole links with magnificent natural features comprising sandwarrens, bold natural plateaux, rough hollows and imposing hazards, which together make any golfer think before he strikes the ball". Apart from mentally adding "she" to that description, it would be hard to better it. This is a wonderful natural links. It's looked after like the national treasure it is. Martin Lipsett, the head greenkeeper, mindful this is one of only 150 links courses in the world, is enhancing the natural links features of the course. It is a pleasure to play golf on fine springy turf, smell the wild flowers, hear the larks, and set foot on natural greens. No grasses imported from the US to usurp the native species. Only organic fertiliser is used. This is how golf courses used to be before television made us believe there is a uniform shade for greens. Grasses naturally grow and die. On Arklow's greens the ball runs true. These greens are fast and firm. All the green-keeping staff are given membership of the club. They are sent to St Andrews to learn how to manage a natural links course. The bunkers are revetted (backed by layered turf) in the St Andrews' style. Wild roses grow here. Larks nest in the rough. The marram grass that grows naturally in the dunes has been carefully transplanted to the two additional holes – making 20 holes in all. Do not be fooled by the inauspicious setting between the Roadstone factory and the Arklow Potteries. This is a wonderful golf course. Before your round, you can look over the lie of the land from the clubhouse, which sits above the course. After your round, you can review the course from the bar. You are assured of a warm welcome, but come on a weekday. This is a popular course. It can be difficult to get a weekend slot.

BEYOND THE 18TH GREEN

The largest natural feature in **West Wicklow** is the huge **Poulaphouca** (Poll an Phúca – "Pool of the Sprite") reservoir formed by the damming of the **River Liffey** at **Blessington** to supply Dublin with water and generate hydro-electricity. **Mullaghcleevaun Mountain** (Mullach Cliabhain – "Summit of the Cradle") one of the highest mountains in the Wicklow range, rises above the eastern shores of the reservoir. You can look across the water to the seventeenth-century coaching town of **Blessington** (Baile Coimín – "Comyn's Town") and the Palladian splendour of **Russborough House**.

The German-born architect Richard Castle (Cassels) designed **Russborough House** for the first Earl of Milltown in 1741. (Castle had just finished work on the Newry canal – the first inland canal in the British Isles.) The central, silvery grey, granite block flanked by curved colonnades, is 275metres/301yards long. The interior is decorated with stucco work by the Francini brothers. It is a magnificent setting for the art collection of Sir Alfred and Lady **Beit** who bought the house in 1951. The collection includes paintings by **Velasquez**, **Murillo**, **Rubens**, **Gainsborough**, **Reynolds**, **Goya** and **Guardi**. (House and collection open May to September, daily 10.30am–5.30pm. Sundays and bank holidays in April and October, and Easter Friday, 10.30–5.30pm. Telephone: 045 865239)

The R756 crosses the **Wicklow Mountains** from west to east. This stretch of road through the 478metre/1569ft high **Wicklow Gap** is one of the best roads in the county. (It was improved and resurfaced for the opening stages of the Tour de France when it came to Ireland in 1998.)

The narrow, wooded valley of **Glendalough** (Gleann dá Locha – "Glen of the Two Lakes") lies below the gap. Here, where the river links two lakes, are the evocative remains – a high (33metre/110ft) round tower, Celtic cross, cathedral and seven small ruined churches – of the great monastic school founded in AD545 by Saint Kevin. The site is filled with the sound of wind in the trees, and the smell of ancient box hedges. **Saint Kevin's Church** has a corbelled roof and was built in the eleventh century on the site of an earlier wooden church. If you are very agile you can walk up to the narrow cave called **Saint Kevin's Bed** on the cliff above the upper lake, where the saint had his hermitage before the churches were built. There are many beautiful walks in the valley. The **Visitor Centre** explains life in an early Christian monastery. (Site always open. Visitor Centre open daily mid-October to mid March 9.30am–5pm; mid-March to May 9.30am–6pm; June to August 9am–6.30pm; September to mid-October 9.30–6pm. Tel: 0404 45325.)

Avondale House, south of **Rathdrum**, was the birthplace and home of the Irish patriot **Charles Stewart Parnell** (1846–1891) who fought for land rights and Home Rule. The plain, square neoclassical house is bowed at the back. The surrounding estate is now **Avondale Forest Park**. (Grounds always open. House open daily March to October 11am–5pm. Telephone: 0404 46111)

The magical, sleeping-beauty world of the wild garden and **Arboretum** at **Kilmacurragh** (signposted on the R752 east from **Rathdrum**) is slowly being restored by **Dúchas** (the Heritage Service). The garden was created in the 19th century – when botanical specimens were being collected from all over the world – by the curator of the National Botanic Gardens at Glasnevin in Dublin, Sir Frederick Moore, his father David Moore, and Thomas Acton who owned the estate. Plants that were also planted at Glasnevin thrived here when they failed at Glasnevin. The rhododendron walk, behind the Queen Anne House (sadly gutted by fire) forms a romantic and magnificent aisle of crimson blossoms in May and June. Old roses trail through the undergrowth. Rare trees abound. It is a lovely place to walk through and picnic in. (Open all year 10am to 5pm)

MEETING OF THE WATERS

"There is not in this wide world a valley so sweet
As that vale in whose bosom the bright waters meet;
Oh! The last rays of feeling and life must depart
Ere the bloom of that valley shall fade from my heart.

Sweet vale of Avoca! How calm could I rest
In thy bosom of shade, with the friends I love best;
Where the storms that we feel in this cold
world should cease,
And your heart, like thy waters, be mingled in peace."
Thomas Moore (1779–1852)

Glendalough

Thomas Moore, one of Ireland's best-known poet/songwriters, is commemorated where the **Avonmore** (Abhainn Mhór – "Big River") and **Avonbeg** (Abhainn Bheag – "Little River") meet in the winding, tree-lined **Vale Of Avoca** (Abhóca) between **Rathdrum** and **Woodenbridge**. Below the bridge which spans the **Avonmore** is a tree stump where the poet is supposed to have sat to compose

"The Meeting of the Waters". The oldest working mill in Ireland is in the village of **Avoca**. (Signposted **Avoca Handweavers**. Open daily, late May to October) There is a second, even lovelier meeting of the waters at **Woodenbridge** (Garrán an Ghabháin – "The Grove of the River-fork") where three rivers – **Aughrim**, **Avoca** and **Gold Mine** – and their valleys unite. As the latter name suggests, gold was mined here in the eighteenth century.

The **Avoca** waters flow into the sea at **Arklow**. The Vikings named **Arklow** – "Arnkell's Meadow". Its Irish name is An tInbhear Mór – "The Big Estuary". It's a resort, with safe, sandy beaches north and south of the river, but it was once an important port. The **Arklow Maritime Museum** tells the story of the town's fishing, boat-building and smuggling past and has a collection of model ships built by sailors on passage in the 18th, 19th and 20th centuries. (Open daily 10am–1pm and 2pm–5pm. Telephone: 0402 32868)

The ruins of a twelfth-century Norman castle, stronghold of the Earls of Ormonde, overlook the Avoca River. A monument marks the spot where Father Murphy, of Boolavogue, the Wexford leader of the 1798 Rebellion, led a band of rebels into battle here, and was killed along with most of his poorly equipped followers.

There are fine, sandy beaches along the coast north from here. The finest of them is **Brittas Bay**.

Baltinglass (Bealach Conglais – "The Road of Cúglais") is on the **River Slaney**. There is an Iron Age hill fort, with a prehistoric chambered cairn, 27metres/90ft in diameter on **Baltinglass Hill** 383metres/1258ft above the river. The cairn contains five burial chambers including a chamber with a decorated basin-stone at the end of a 4metre/12ft passage. The view from the top of the hill is worth the climb. The ruined chapel and cloisters of twelfth-century **Baltinglass Abbey** overlook the river. It was founded by Dermot MacMurrough, King of Leinster. The R747 from **Baltinglass** to **Arklow** crosses briefly into **County Carlow**, and across some very pretty valleys. **Aughrim** (Eachdhroim – "Horse Ridge") lies where several mountain valleys meet and two rivers join to form the **Aughrim River**. A road into the mountains leads to **Lughaquilla** (Log na Coille – "Hollow of the Wood") – the highest mountain in the Wicklow range (925metres/3039ft).

If you're a fair weather golfer, if you want to check your technique, or if you want a tour of the best-known North American courses, you can play **Virtual Golf** at **Moneylands Farm**. The sun is always shining on the **Golf Simulator**. And it's great fun. (Telephone: 0402 32259)

TOURIST INFORMATION

Fitzwilliam Square, Wicklow
Telephone: 0404 69117
Main Street, Arklow (June to September)
Telephone: 0402 32484

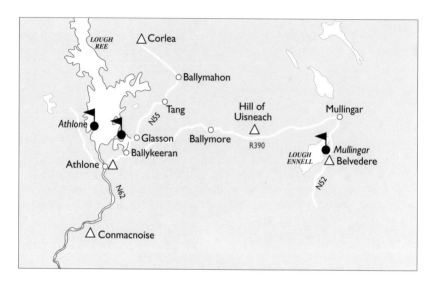

(Golf Courses: Mullingar, Glasson and Athlone)

Distances: Athlone to Mullingar 46km/28.5miles; Athlone to Glasson 10km/6miles; Athlone to Corlea 34km/21miles.

In the Midlands of Ireland the land never rises higher than 259metres/850ft, but if you climb one of the low hills between Lough Ree and Lough Ennell, you will see a surprisingly varied landscape of island-studded lakes, winding rivers, forest, bog, quiet roads and green pastures. One of these hills is Uisneach, the very centre of Ireland. It was the seat of the high kings – "where Malachy wore the collar of gold". The golf courses, in lovely, rolling lakeland settings, are among the best inland courses in Ireland.

MULLINGAR
18 holes – par 72 (5913metres/6468yards)
At Belvedere, on the N52, south of Mullingar.
Green Fees: IR£20 weekdays, IR£25 weekends and bank holidays.
Telephone: 044 48366

Glasson Golf Course

The illustrious James Braid laid out Mullingar golf club in 1937. It fans out from the splendid clubhouse in two loops of nine. The members say Mullingar is easy. The visitor playing here for the first – or even the second and third – time is unlikely to agree. It's hillier than you might expect in the Midlands. There are blind tee-shots and blind approaches to greens, and it can be difficult to judge distance. There are not too many fairway bunkers but where they exist they are strategically placed, and the raised greens are well bunkered. Mature oaks and beeches, and new planting provide additional hazards. The holes are long and the fairways generous, with a ditch to carry on the 10th and 16th. You can get your woods out and open your shoulders. For ladies there are some long carries to the fairways – six par 5s! There are four par 5s on the men's card (three of them on the back nine). The 7th is a long par 4 (par 5 for ladies) and bunkers left and right of the green make the approach shot particularly difficult. The most challenging holes on the first nine are two long par 3s played across valleys to well guarded greens that are hard to hold. (The 2nd was chosen by Christy O'Connor senior in a best-of-Ireland selection.) The 8th is a fiendishly bunkered par 4. The 17th is a terrific dogleg left from an elevated tee. Trees guard the corner on the left, out-of-bounds Belvedere estate is over the hedge on the right as you hit up to a well-defended plateau green. The ground is springy underfoot and the greens are excellent. You'll enjoy your golf at Mullingar.

GLASSON
18 holes – par 72
10km/6miles north of Athlone on the N55.
Green Fees: IR£30 Monday to Thursday, IR£32 Friday,
Sunday and bank holidays, IR£35 Sunday.
Telephone: 0902 85120

When you meet visiting golfers on other courses in the Midlands they ask, "Have you played Glasson yet?" It's the kind of course you want to recommend to the next golfer you meet. It lies on the peninsula that encloses Killinure Bay in Lough Ree – part of the long Shannon River system. The first nine holes overlook the Lough and Hare Island, the second nine are on the shores of Killinure Bay. You need to keep to the right off the tee at the opening par 4 on the slopes above the clubhouse. You can then let rip for a par 5 over the same gently rolling terrain. The 3rd is a super par 3 from a raised tee to a plateau green – the entrance defended by three bunkers. The view is of lovely, wooded, Hare Island in Lough Ree. The challenge is to reach the green in the face of the wind that blows from the west across the lough. The 5th is another cunningly bunkered par 3. At the 6th you encounter the first of five ponds introduced by the designer, Christy O'Connor Junior. It lies to the right of the fairway on this par 5. To the left is out-of-bounds all the way to the green. Enjoy the splendid views from the 7th green at the top of a hill. The downhill 8th (par 4) doglegs left to a green with a pond curving along the left-hand side and around the back, and a bunker on the right. The 9th brings you back uphill again to the centre of the course. It is worth climbing to the back tees, enclosed in a copse of trees, high above the fairway on the 14th for the magnificent view over Killinure Bay. The hole – the longest at 517metres/566yards from these blue tees – turns sharp right at a bunker and is downhill again – bunkers on the left, ponds on the right – to the green by the lough shore. Have a look from the back tees on the 15th (par 3) as well. From here, the carry over the lough to the promontory green is 169metres/185yards. Glasson, however, with four tees at every hole, provides for all levels of ability. For ladies, the carry over the lough at the 15th is a manageable 105metres/115yards – but beware the wind from the lough. The 16th is a long and tough par 4. Water threatens your drive. Bunkers narrow the fairway before rising to a platform green defended by two more bunkers. Two more terrific par 4s complete the round in front of the Georgian clubhouse – formerly the home of Glasson's owners, the Reid family. Before tackling this scenic, always interesting and challenging parkland course, you can loosen up on three practice holes – as beautifully maintained as the course itself.

ATHLONE
18 holes – par 71 (5973metres/6537yards)
Hodson Bay. Signposted from N61 north of Athlone.
Green Fees: IR£18 weekdays, IR£20 weekends and bank holidays.
Telephone: 0902 92073

How lush, how green, how mature is this lovely course on a peninsula in Lough Ree – the trees are particularly beautiful. They are nearly all native hardwoods – ash, beech, oak, lime and chestnut. They line the fairways, and curve along the shores of the lough. The course has water on three sides. The fairways invite your drives, the slopes and contours challenge you to place the ball accurately – particularly on the 2nd (par 3). The land slopes steeply left between tee and green. A short, narrow platform of fairway runs along the high boundary fence on the right between you and the road. The only haven is the green. The 4th tee (par 4) lies between two gravelly ridges. The land is flatter here. As you walk down the fairway, you glimpse the lake through the trees on your right, across the fairways on your left, and in the distance ahead. The wind that blows across the lough comes into play. You are now on the most exposed part of the course. The 6th tee is set back, close to the shore. On this dogleg to the right, three left-hand bunkers guard the corner. The lake cuts in sharply on the right, narrowing the fairway. This is a short, but tricky par 5 for men and a very tough par 4 for ladies. The 8th fairway, gently curving right and rising to the green, particularly invites you to open your shoulders and let fly. But watch out for the tall ash tree, which guards the bottom of the slope. This par 4 (par 5 for ladies) is not as easy as it looks. The 12th is an astonishing par 4 (par 5 for ladies). Beneath the elevated tee is a deep gully that descends like a ski-slope from a ridge between two mounds. Your tee-shot over the ridge is blind. If you drive straight over the ridge, you then face a blind second shot from another alpine depression, over a second ridge at 90 degrees angle to the tee. If you ignore the advice printed in the course guide – "An iron off the tee for the longer hitters" – and land in the deep rough, high above the fairway, you will at least see the green, guarded by a

Athlone

sand bunker and a grass bunker, at the end of this roller coaster. You will not forget the 12th at Athlone. Nor will you forget the lovely lakeside 16th – a long par 4 (412metres/453yards from the medal tees). Trees line the fairway and curve around the back of the green, which falls away towards them. The fairway

doglegs left and is narrowed by the trees as it rises to the green. The finishing hole is both beautiful and tough – a drive through an avenue of tall trees then a shot up to the green in front of the clubhouse. There are panoramic views from the bar and dining room over the course and Lough Ree.

BEYOND THE 18TH GREEN

Athlone (Baile Átha Luain – "Town of Luan's Ford") is a lovely town on the River Shannon, just down river from Lough Ree (Loch Rí – "King's Lake"). Boats and cabin cruisers are moored on either side of the **Town Bridge** across the Shannon. The Old Irish name of the town was Áth Mór ("Great Ford") because it was one of the most important and strategic crossings of the river. The ford was defended by the tribes of cattle-rich Leinster against the western tribes of Connacht. In 1001 the High King of Ireland, Brian Boru, sailed his fleet up the Shannon to a great feast at Athlone. King Turlough O'Connor built the first bridge in 1129. The Anglo-Norman, John de Gray, Bishop of Norwich built **Athlone Castle**.
It was the last stronghold of the Irish after their defeat at the Battle of the Boyne in the Williamite Wars (1690–1691). The **Visitor Centre** in the castle tells the story of the Siege of Athlone, the **Military History** of the town, the Irish tenor **Count John McCormack** (the town's most famous son), and the **River Shannon**. (Visitor Centre open May to October 9.30am–5.30pm. Telephone: 0902 92912)

Clonmacnoise, the most beautiful and important of Ireland's monastic sites, on a bend of the **Shannon** is best approached from the river. **Clonmacnoise** (Cluain Mic Nois – "Pasture of the Descendants of Noas") was founded by Saint Ciaran, who left his hermitage on **Hare Island** in **Lough Ree** and came to here in AD545. Ireland became known as the "Island of Saints and Scholars" because of the fame and influence of Clonmacnoise. Its riches and reputation attracted Viking invaders who plundered it repeatedly. In 1170, Darbforgaill (Dervorgilla), who was abducted from her husband by Diarmait MacMurchada (Dermot MacMurrough), retired here in penance. (The Normans invaded Ireland when Dermot MacMurrough called in Strongbow to support him against his rivals, including Dervorgilla's angry husband.) It was finally destroyed and vandalised during the Elizabethan wars when the English garrison at **Athlone** took everything that could be carried, including the glass from the windows. The 18metre/60ft defensive **Round Tower** and the **Cross of the Scriptures** date from the tenth century. There are also the ruins of a cathedral, seven churches, two round towers, three high crosses and a castle. **Clonmacnoise** is very popular with visitors, particularly during July and August. (Open daily 9am–7pm mid-May to mid-September, 10am–6pm mid-September to November, 10am–5.30pm November to mid-March, 10am–6pm mid-March to mid-May. Telephone: 0905 74195)

Viking Tours sail down river to **Clonmacnoise** and up river to **Lough Ree** from **Athlone**. The journey and tour of **Clonmacnoise** takes about four hours. There are regular tours of **Lough Ree** and return trips to **Hodson Bay**. (Daily trips May to September; April to October on request. Telephone: 086 262 1136. Tickets on departure from **Strand Fishing Tackle** just below the town bridge. Telephone: 0902 79277)

On the N55 from **Athlone** to **Glasson** (Glasán – "Little Stream") just past **Ballykeeran** (Bealach Caorthainn – "Pass of the Rowan Tree") there is a lookout over Lough Ree, its islands and inner loughs. The area between Glasson and Tang (Teanga – "Tongue") is associated with playwright **Oliver Goldsmith** (1728–1774) and there is now a signposted **Goldsmith Trail** around the sites which feature in "The Deserted Village":

> *"Sweet Auburn! Loveliest village of the plain*
> *Where health and plenty cheered the labouring swain,*
> *Where smiling spring its earliest visit paid,*
> *And parting summer's lingering blooms delayed:"*

Glasson, also known as "The Village of the Roses", is believed by some scholars to be Goldsmith's "Sweet Auburn". **The Pinnacle** – a circular structure on a hill about 2km/1.25miles along the road from **Glasson** to **Kilkenny West** (where Goldsmith's father and brother were rectors) is said to mark the exact geographical centre of Ireland. It was built by Nathaniel Lowe in 1769 as a signalling tower.

Oliver Goldsmith was born near **Ballymahon** (Baile uí Mhathaín – "Ó Mathaín's Townland"). Further north, **Corlea Trackway** and **Visitor Centre** displays part of an Iron Age road found uncovered during turf cutting in 1984 and dated to 148BC. The road is made of great planks of oak, like railway sleepers, on runners of birch and ash. Marks show it carried wheeled traffic. It's thought to be part of an Iron Age road system that connected Cruachain (the ancient capital of Connacht) with the **Hill of Uisneach** about 32km/20miles away. (It may even have continued to the **Hill of Tara** 80km/50miles away.) Guided tours take visitors on to the surrounding bog to explain the ecology and point out interesting bog features such as the insect-eating sundew plant. A film shows how the road was discovered and preserved, and a specially built room displays a section of the road. (Open daily 10am–6pm April to September. Telephone: 043 22386)

The R390 from **Athlone** to **Mullingar** (An Muileann gCearr – "Crooked Mill") is a quiet, pretty road through gently rolling countryside. In ancient times, this was the route between **Uisneach** and **Athlone**.

Modern Ireland has four provinces – Ulster, Munster, Leinster and Connacht. Ancient Ireland had a fifth province, Mide, the Middle Kingdom, ruled from **Tara**. (The name survives in the county names of Meath and Westmeath.) The five ancient provinces met at the **Hill of Uisneach** (210metres/690ft) about halfway between **Athlone** and **Mullingar**. (Look out for a sign and a wicket gate about 7km/4miles west of **Ballymore**) You can see for miles from the top of the hill. A 6metre/19ft high limestone rock known as **Aill na Mireann** or the **Catstone** (because it looks like a crouching cat) is said to mark the actual point on the hill where the five provinces met. The **Hill of Uisneach** was the site of the great pagan festival of **Bealtaine**, which marked the beginning of the season that ran from May Day to Lughnasa (the harvest festival at the end of August.) This was when the cattle were driven from winter to summer pastures – a custom known as booleying. The **Bealtaine** festival rituals were designed to protect the livestock from disease. Cattle were driven between two great fires to the accompaniment of incantations. (There is an old Irish saying Idir dhá tine la Bhealtaine – "between the two fires of Bealtaine" similar to the English "between a rock and a hard place".) King Tuathal Teachtmhair in the second century inaugurated a yearly meeting of chieftains at the Bealtaine Festival. (It lasted about two weeks and was attended by traders from the Mediterranean.) Traces of King Tuathal's fortress can be seen on the eastern summit of the hill.

Mullingar, between **Lough Owel** (Loch Uair – "Uair's Lake") and **Lough Ennell** (Loch Ainnínne – "Ainneanne's Lake") is the county town and a centre for the beef cattle trade that is still an important part of the local economy. **Belvedere House** beside **Mullingar Golf Club** about 6km/4miles south of the town was built by the famous German-born architect **Richard Castle** (Cassels) in 1740 as a fishing lodge for **Robert Rochfort** the first **Lord Belvedere**. It has the finest stucco ceilings in Ireland. Three flights of broad stone terracing lead from the house to the lake, ornamental gardens and landscaped parkland. Near the house stands the largest and most spectacular folly in Ireland – **The Jealous Wall** – a faux Gothic ruin which **Robert Rochfort** built in 1760 to block the view of the nearby house and estate belonging to his brother George with whom he had quarrelled. He was also vindictive and cruel to his wife **Mary Molesworth** whom he accused of adultery with his younger brother, Arthur, and locked up in the family house while he lived a bachelor's life at **Belvedere**. His wife remained imprisoned for thirty-one years. These stories of jealousy, passion and revenge are dramatically reconstructed in an audio-visual display at the **Visitor Centre**. (House, gardens and park open daily 10.30am–8pm April to August, 10.30am–6.30pm September to October, 10.30am–4.30pm November to March. Telephone: 044 49060)

TOURIST INFORMATION

Athlone Tourist Office: Athlone Castle, Athlone, County Westmeath
Telephone: 0902 94630
Mullingar Tourist Office: Market Square, Mullingar, County Westmeath
Telephone: 044 48650

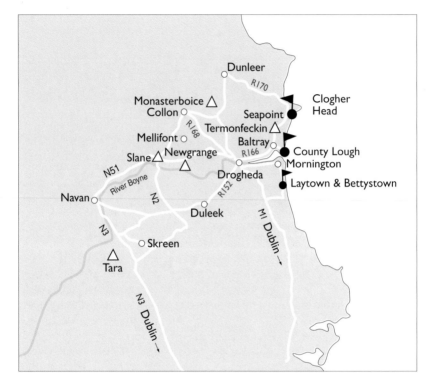

(Golf Courses: County Louth (Baltray), Seapoint, Laytown and Bettystown)

Distances: Drogheda to Slane 14km/8.5miles; Slane to Navan 14km/8.5miles; Navan to Trim 14.5km/9miles; Navan to Tara 8km/5miles; Drogheda to Clogherhead 13km/8miles.

The land around the estuary and along the wide, slow-flowing and beautiful River Boyne, is full of riches – fertile farmland, archaeological treasures, fine scenery, and some of the most beautiful Celtic high crosses in Ireland. Much of Ireland's history is written on the landscape here – from the Hill of Tara and the Lia Fáil (Stone of Destiny) to the plain where the Battle of the Boyne decided the subsequent course of Irish politics. The loop of the River Boyne between the pretty village of Slane and the port of Drogheda contains some of the most important cultural sites in Ireland and is a UNESCO World Heritage Zone. It is a little known fact that a golfer from this part of the world – Arthur Mulligan – instituted the "Mulligan" – a free stroke allowed each player on each nine holes of a friendly match, to be used at the player's discretion. (The "provisional Mulligan" is a less-well known variation of the stroke.)

COUNTY LOUTH
18 holes – par 73 (6198metres/6783yards)
On the R167 8km/5miles northeast of Drogheda between Baltray and Termonfeckin.
Green Fees: IR£50 weekdays, IR£60 weekends.
Telephone: 041 982 2329

As you park beside the clubhouse and survey the links you wonder what all the fuss is about. At first sight Baltray, as it is usually called, is flat and featureless. But there is more rise and fall in the land than at first sight. Softly undulating links land ripples out from the clubhouse towards a long, low line of dunes. No towering sand-hills here. Yet this is a subtle and testing course. Golfers talk about Baltray as wine buffs talk about a grand cru. It is a favourite with golf connoisseurs. There are a lot of them about, because to play Baltray you need to book well in advance. It is among the top-ranked courses in the British Isles. It was first laid out in 1892 but didn't achieve greatness until Tom Simpson (architect of Cruden Bay in Scotland) and his assistant Molly Gourlay redesigned it in 1937. It's fitting that a woman's hand helped mould Baltray, because it nurtured two outstanding women amateurs, Clarrie Tiernan and the legendary Philomena Garvey – 15 times Irish Ladies' champion, 7 times Curtis Cup player (1946–60), and British Ladies' champion 1957 (4 times runner-up). The redesigned course was opened by another golfing legend – James Bruen. Baltray is always fair. There is only one blind shot – the approach to the narrow green, down by the Boyne estuary, on the 3rd (par 5) is over a narrow ridge. The 3rd, 4th and 14th are bunker free. Natural bumps and hollows determine the placing of shots. Elsewhere, the bunkers are perfectly sited to catch mistakes. Accuracy is particularly rewarded on the 5th – a par 3 where the only place to land your ball is on the green. The greens are like silk. They repay close study and a very light touch. There is not much shelter so the wind is always a factor. The 12th and 13th are difficult holes through the dunes with narrow approaches to the greens. You can hear the sea pounding the beach behind the ridge of sand-hills on your right. From the back of the red tees on the 13th you can see the sweep of a small bay, the fishing village of Baltray and the distant Mournes. (Slieve Binnian is shaped like a head and shoulders. Slieve Donard, which looms over Royal County Down, is the tallest peak.) The beautiful, bunkerless 14th has a downhill tee-shot and a pitch up to a plateau green which falls away on three sides and is hard to hold. The finishing hole is a well-bunkered par 5. Baltray is a busy course. Avoid weekends and Tuesdays and Wednesdays after 11.30am.

SEAPOINT
18 holes – par 72 (6339metres/6937yards)
At Termonfeckin on the R166 between Drogheda and Clogherhead.
Green Fees: summer IR£25 weekdays and bank holidays, IR£30 weekends; winter IR£30 weekdays and bank holidays, IR£35 weekends.
Telephone: 041 98 22333

Seapoint costs more to play in winter because it stays open all year round and promises no recourse to temporary tees and greens. Yet this is not completely a links course. The front nine, away from the sea, have a definite parkland, even American, look. Water comes into play on the 1st, 2nd, 4th, 5th and 6th. It is most dramatically dangerous on the 5th where the natural stream that defines the western perimeter of the course has been diverted into three ponds. This is the toughest hole on the course. Go to the back tees and look at the awe-inspiring tee-shot over all three ponds, fringed with tall bulrushes. You will see why Seapoint was chosen to host the Irish PGA championship. (Lesser men and ladies have at least one pond less to carry.) The 6th is a dogleg right over another pond from a tee-box enclosed by trees. But it looks and plays like a links hole, with small dunes running up the right-hand side of the fairway to a mound-enclosed green. Most of the fairways on the opening nine are re-sown with the bent and fescue grasses of natural links land. You catch the first sight of the sea over a low ridge of dunes to the left of the 10th. The 11th doglegs right through gorse-lined dunes to an elevated, tiered green. The 14th is a particularly lovely hole with a difficult uphill approach to the green, secluded in trees with tall pines at the back. Wild roses line the pathway to the 15th – a par 3 to a green that falls away to the left. And then you are back-to-back with Baltray on the 16th tee, the beach running along the right-hand side of the fairway below you. You have a real risk of landing on the beach on the 17th (par 3) if the wind is blowing from the west. Avoid the pot bunker on the right as you play a fine par 5 finish along the dunes and the sea to the clubhouse. This is a course that doesn't let you down at the end.

LAYTOWN AND BETTYSTOWN
18 holes – par 71 (5852metres/6405yards)
Bettystown, County Meath.
Green Fees: IR£25 weekdays, IR£30 weekends and bank holidays.
Telephone: 041 98 27563

This is a testing links, particularly when the wind blows hard along the coast. It demands are clear from the 1st tee where men are faced with a long carry over two mounds and the greenkeeper's hut in the hollow between them. The course

Seapoint Golf Course, Termonfeckin

is laid out in a long rectangle of land between a ridge of dunes behind the strand, and the coast road. Most of the front nine are played along the shoreline, through the dunes, and most of the back nine are played on slightly flatter land nearer the road. The lies are very tight. The greens are fast. The terrain has all the hummocks and hollows of the classic links, the fairways fall away left or right into deep rough. Sometimes – as on the 2nd – they slope both ways. At least the long carries demanded here, and on the 3rd and 4th, will usually have the prevailing wind behind them. The 5th is a memorable dogleg right around sand-hills. You drive to the fairway and then see what appears to be a huge mound (in fact it's a series of mounds) at the entrance to the plateau green. There is rough to left and right. It's a relief to see a par 3 next. The 7th demands another long carry from the men's tee through a narrow opening to the fairway, guarded by a tree. (You have a great view along the coast from the platform tee.) There is never a dull hole. Just when you think the roller coaster through the dunes has ended and you contemplate the relatively flatter holes nearer the road, up come three long, tough, well-bunkered par 4s – 11th 12th and 13th – played into the prevailing wind. The 12th (421metres/461yards from the back tees) is an easier par 5 for ladies. There is only one – very inviting – par 3 on this back nine (the 16th). The 18th is a dogleg par 5 with another long carry to the fairway, which turns sharply left. The green is glimpsed through a gap in the encircling hummocks. A ditch runs along the right-hand side. A memorable finish.

The twin resorts of **Laytown** (An Inse – "The Holm") and **Bettystown** (Baile an Bhiataigh – "Betagh's Townland") are connected by an 8km/5mile long beach. This is where one of the most important archaeological finds in Ireland – the Tara Brooch – was made in 1850. (The gold and bronze brooch with intricate filigree settings of semi-precious stones, enamel and glass, in the classic pin and circle shape of Celtic jewellery is on display in the National Museum in Dublin.) **Laytown** is famous for its annual race meeting on the strand – the only beach races in the world run under Jockey Club rules. The race meeting is usually around the time of the June bank holiday.

The tall, square, crenellated sixteenth-century **Mornington Tower**, which you can see from Laytown and Bettystown golf course, was built to warn shipping entering **Drogheda** harbour.

Drogheda (Droichead Átha – "Bridge of the Ford") was captured by the Vikings in the early tenth century and by the Normans in the thirteenth century. Kezar's Lane is a reminder of the Viking past and **St Lawrence's Gate** (part of the thirteenth-century barbican) is a relic of the Norman past. But it is two names from the religious wars of the seventeenth century that are most associated with the town. In 1649 it was captured by Oliver Cromwell who slaughtered more than 3,000 of its inhabitants – including women, children and priests – claiming the "righteous judgement of God upon those barbarous wretches". Oliver Plunkett was the Catholic Archbishop of Armagh and Primate of Ireland. He spent much of his ministry in hiding because of the Penal Laws against Catholics. He was hanged, drawn and quartered at Tyburn (near Marble Arch) in London in 1681 after being falsely accused of taking part in a "popish plot" and was declared a saint in 1975. His head is preserved in a shrine in **St Peter's Church** – built in his memory after Catholic emancipation in the nineteenth century. The award-winning town **Museum** is housed in the early nineteenth-century military barracks and martello tower on **Millmount** – a grassy mound on the south side of the river overlooking the town – built on the site of a Norman motte and bailey, and possibly a Bronze Age passage graves system. (Museum open daily. Monday to Saturday 10am–5pm, Sunday and bank holidays 2pm–5pm. Telephone: 041 983 3097) The **Drogheda Heritage Route** is a signposted walk around the town. (Map from the tourist office at the bus depot on the corner of Donore Road. Telephone: 041 983 7070)

The coast road, north of **Drogheda**, takes you through **Baltray** (Baile na Trá – "Town of the Strand") and **Termonfeckin** (Tearmann Féichín – St Feichin's Sanctuary Land") to the pretty fishing village, strand and rocky cliffs at **Clogherhead** (Clochar – "Stony Place"). **Termonfeckin Castle** has a four-storied tower and spiral staircase. A ninth-century **High Cross** in the Church of Ireland graveyard is deemed to mark the site of a sixth-century church. The present church was designed by **Francis Johnston** (1760–1829) architect of the GPO and the Bank of Ireland in Dublin. All the graves in the tranquil churchyard face the sea. On leaving **Termonfeckin** take the alternative route for **Clogherhead** via **Castlecoohill** (103metres/313ft) for a fine view north along the coast to the **Cooley Mountains** and the **Mountains of Mourne**.

The three high crosses in the small, quiet site at **Monasterboice** (Mainistir Bhuithe – "St Buithe's Monastery") are said to be the finest in Ireland (some say Europe) and the **Saint Muiredach's** or the **South Cross** (5metres/17ft high) is the finest of the three. **Saint Muiredach** was the abbot here from 890 to 923. (An inscription on the base of the cross says: "A prayer for Muiredach by whom this cross was made.") The round tower is ninth century, and is the tallest in Ireland (110metres/358ft). The larger of two ruined churches dates from the eighth century. The name of the River Boyne (Bóinne) may be derived from St Buithe. (Always open. Signposted from the N1 north of **Drogheda**.)

Mellifont Abbey (An Mhainistir Mhór – "The Great Monastery") – the first Cistercian foundation in Ireland (1142) stands in the tranquil valley of a tributary of the Boyne. Only the square **Gate House** still stands, but there are also the graceful ruins of the fourteenth-century **Chapter House**, the thirteenth-century octagonal **Lavabo** and the Romanesque cloister. Following its confiscation in the dissolution of the monasteries by Henry VIII, it became a residence until the early eighteenth century. **William of Orange** made it his headquarters before the **Battle of the Boyne** (1690). (Site always open.)

A big orange and green sign beside the river near **Tullyallen** (Tulaich Álainn – "Lovely Hill") marks the **Battlefield of the Boyne** where King Billy (William of Orange) triumphed over the deposed **King James II**. Signs show where the armies camped, where King William crossed the river and where the battle was fought. Although it was not the end of the Jacobite and Catholic cause in Ireland (that came when the Treaty of Limerick was broken in 1691) it signalled the end. That's why it's celebrated every year by the Protestant Orange Order.

This is where the **Boyne** loops south and encompasses the treasures of **Brú na Bóinne** (Bend of the Boyne) – the remarkable and mysterious passage graves of **Newgrange**, **Knowth** and **Dowth**. These are curved mounds on a ridge above the Boyne. The jewel of **Brú na Bóinne** is **Newgrange** (Sí an Bhrú). The mound, covered with water-rolled white quartz pebbles, pre-dates the pyramids by centuries and Stonehenge by a thousand years. The stone at the entrance is carved with spirals and diamond shapes. The guided tour takes you down the 19metre/63ft narrow passage to the cruciform shaped central burial chamber decorated with whorls and spirals. The opening was built to allow the rays of the rising sun at the winter solstice to enter a precisely aligned slit, move slowly down the passage and flood the chamber with light. There is a ten-year waiting list to experience this phenomenon. In the meantime, make do with the electric recreation of the event that is part of the daily tours. The two burial chambers at **Knowth** (separate tour) have the richest collection of megalithic art in Europe. One chamber has a magnificently decorated stone ritual basin. (**Dowth** is still being excavated and is not open to the public.) **Brú na Bóinne** is one of the most visited sites in Ireland. Avoid weekends in July and August if possible. Allow an hour for the **Visitor Centre**, two hours for the **Centre** and **Newgrange** or **Knowth**, three hours for the **Centre**, **Newgrange** and **Knowth**. The last tour is 90 minutes before closing; the last admission to the centre is 45 minutes before closing. (Opening times: June to mid-September 9am–7pm; May and mid- to end-September 9am–6.30pm; March, April and October 9.30am–5.30pm; November to February 9.30am–5pm. **Newgrange** open all year. **Knowth** open May to October. Telephone: 0141 988 0300)

Slane (Baile Shláine – "Townland of Fullness") lies beneath the **Hill of Slane** (161metres/529ft) where Saint Patrick symbolically lit the paschal fire, in defiance of the pagan High King of Tara, and then converted the king, and thus Ireland, to Christianity.

The **Ledwidge Cottage Museum** commemorates the poet **Francis Ledwidge** (1891–1917) who was killed at Ypres in Flanders in 1917. Although he fought with the Royal Inniskilling Fusiliers, he felt the tug of Irish Nationalism too. His best-known poem is a lament for Thomas McDonagh, written only days after McDonagh – a fellow poet and one of the signatories of the Irish Declaration of Independence – was executed in May 1916 for his part in the Easter Rising.

> *"He shall not hear the bittern cry*
> *In the wild sky, where he is lain,*
> *Nor voices of the sweeter birds*
> *Above the wailing of the rain."*

The poet Seamus Heaney, in an essay about Ledwidge, observed how the bridge over the Boyne in **Slane** divides the two Irelands inhabited by Ledwidge. Upriver, Slane Castle, in the Gothic Revival style of the eighteenth century, stands in the parkland and grounds created by the English garden designer Capability Brown. Downriver, cattle graze in long meadows by the meandering Boyne and distant ruins and round towers are reminders of an earlier, Gaelic Ireland. Both views are charming.

You can see why the **Hill of Tara** (Teamhair na Riogh – "Conspicuous Place of the Kings") was chosen as the seat of the high kings of Ireland. From the top of the hill you can see for miles in every direction. You can even see the weather fronts roll from the far west across the plains of Meath. Sheep graze among the

Opposite page:
Melifont Abbey

earthworks on the hill, which is reached through a churchyard of St Patrick's Church on the side of the hill. There are about a dozen identified mounds, circles and stones. The largest circle is Rath na Riogh (Royal Enclosure). Inside the circle are Dumhna na nGiall (Mound of the Hostages) – a passage grave under a circular mound – and Lia Fáil (Stone of Destiny). The entrance to the Mound of the Hostages is two standing stones and a capstone. The stones lining the interior passage are decorated with carved whorls. When excavated, the tomb contained the largest collection of artefacts found in a passage grave, including bronze daggers, a stone axe, and a necklace dated to 1400BC. You need to spend time wandering over the hill absorbing the atmosphere and imagining the ceremonies and the feasting in the Teach Miodchuarta (The House of Mead Circling, or, Banquet Hall). Only a long, wide hollow is visible, but it was described in early Irish manuscripts as a rectangular wooden hall in which every grade of society had a place, and an appropriate cut of meat – rib of beef for the king and so on down the line. (Site always open. Signposted from the N2 south of **Slane**. Visitor centre open mid-June to mid-September 9.30am–6pm, May to mid-June 10am–6pm, mid-September to end of October 10am–5pm. Telephone: 046 25903)

TOURIST INFORMATION

(East coast and Midlands Tourism)
Bus Eireann Bus Depot, Drogheda
Telephone: 041 983 7070
Jocelyn Street, Dundalk, County Louth
Telephone: 042 933 5484

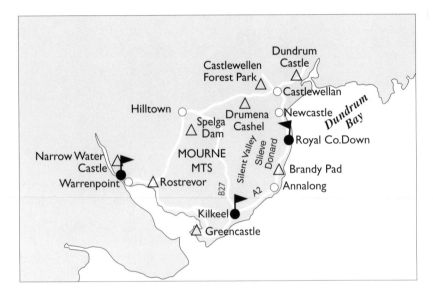

(Golf Courses: Royal County Down, Kilkeel, Warrenpoint.)

Distances: Newcastle to Warrenpoint 40km/25miles; Kilkeel to Hilltown 21km/13miles; Hilltown to Castlewellan 15km/9miles.

The composer Percy French made the Mountains of Mourne world famous when he contrasted the money-seeking world of London with the beauty and simplicity of south County Down "where the Mountains of Mourne sweep down to the sea". On the lower, south-facing slopes, dry-stone walls divide small potato fields. The pattern continues to the water's edge.

The landscape was formed by volcanic eruptions nearly 60 million years ago. The lava cooled to form granite mountains. In the last ice age, glaciers gouged and smoothed the mountains, cutting gaps and valleys and creating the twelve peaks of the Mountains of Mourne (Beanna Boirche – "Peaks of Boirche"). Saint Donart, who brought Christianity to the area, lived in a stone cell on top of the highest mountain, Slieve Donard (Sliabh Dónairt – "Donart's Mountain"). A

37km/22mile wall (built by Belfast Water Commissioners to enclose the reservoir which supplies the city) links all the principal peaks in the Mournes. In the curve of the coast between Newcastle and Warrenpoint, these form the backdrop to some of the most scenic golf courses in Ireland.

ROYAL COUNTY DOWN
Championship Links 18 hole – par 71 (6333metres/7037yards)
Annesley Links 18 holes – par 66 (4213metres/4681yards)
Signposted in the town of Newcastle.
Green Fees: Championship Links October to March £35; April to October £70 weekdays, £80 weekends, Sundays after 4pm £27 to holders of GUI Ulster Branch handicaps. Annesley Links October to March £12 weekdays, £18 Sundays; April to October £16 weekdays, £23 Sundays.
Telephone: 028 43 723314

There are two courses and three clubs on the links land that runs along Dundrum Bay below Slieve Donard. Royal County Down, the men's club, was founded in 1889 by the local landowner, the fifth Earl of Annesley. The ladies' club – the first in Ireland – was founded in 1894 at a time when Irish women were winning every available trophy in the British Isles. The Mourne club was founded for the "townsmen" of Newcastle. All three clubs play on the Championship course and the Annesley course. Mourne can't play the Championship course on Saturdays. Ladies must qualify to play it. Despite these hangovers from the days when class and sex divisions were more rigid, Royal County Down, alone among the great links of Ireland, consciously prices itself within the reach of golfers with modest means. Visitors to the Championship course enjoy low-season and summer-evening rates that are the best value in the British Isles. The shorter, but testing, Annesley links is good value too. The "grand old man" of golf, Old Tom Morris, designed the Championship course – noting the suitability of the ground and "the magnificence of the surrounding scenery". The Ladies'Golf Union first gave it championship status by staging the Ladies' British Amateur Open on it in 1899. (It was won by the youngest ever winner – May Hezlet, from Royal Portrush.) The Annesley course was laid out in 1900. Edward VII conferred the "Royal" title when he visited the club in 1908.

Championship Course: The marketing image is white clouds, blue sky, and the green and gold links stretching along the strand towards the purple mountains. But unless you have been there, you won't know about the scent – the coconut-and-vanilla scent of whins (gorse) mixed with the salty, ozone tang of the sea – that fills the air from spring to autumn. There is nothing like it. Take a deep breath as you prepare to play the sublime gorse-lined 13th and you will know what I mean. Nor can a photograph do justice to bunkers like great golden eyes fringed with giant lashes. Once seen, never forgotten. They really are sand traps.

(You may have to play out backwards.) This is a course whose character is apparent from the start. You set off down a valley in the dune system. The Mountains of Mourne are behind you. The sea is on your right, always within earshot; but you will only glimpse it on these opening holes if you are unlucky enough to land in the sand-hills. The astonishing 2nd hole calls for a blind tee-shot over a ridge to the fairway. From the crest of the ridge you see the approach to the green is through another ridge. The green – on a low plateau – is guarded by a cluster of bunkers and small dunes. Bunkers line up like sentries on either side of the 3rd fairway. Giant sand-hills tower behind the 4th tee and nine bunkers lie in wait for your ball. The 5th is a dogleg right to a green hidden in the dunes. The sequence of astonishing holes continues all the way to the 16th. The most famous view is from the Championship 4th tee but a better sense of the layout and setting is from the 6th tee. The latter requires another blind shot from the tee (there are five altogether). But a shot is only blind the first time, and this is a course to which you will long to return – especially after playing the gorse-lined, curving beauty that is the 13th. The greens are very fast. The rough is penal. Stay on the fairways! Critics say the three closing holes are an anti-climax and the 16th (par 4) is too easy for today's long hitters who can drive the green. But who can deny the pleasure of walking to the tee through gorse as high as trees and then making par or birdie? The bunker eyes watch you all the way up the 18th. You will want to challenge them again.

Annesley Course: Although much shorter than the adjoining Championship course (the only par 5 is on the ladies' card) it is both demanding and great fun to play. You must be accurate. Wild hitters will lose a lot of balls. The opening holes are fairly flat and run along the inland boundary of the links. You first catch sight of the sea on the 5th green. From the 6th to the 14th the course twists and plunges through sand-hills, whins and heather. The fairways are narrow, the greens small. Gorse surrounds the 7th tee. You hit over criss-crossing paths to the short fairway. The 8th winds through a valley in the dunes to a tiny green. At the 10th tee the sea and towering sand-hills lie before you. Behind you, the entire links rolls away towards the mountains. Hold your nerve at the 11th and strike out over a deep gorse-filled hollow to the fairway. The pot bunker on the 12th is perfectly placed. It's the best par 3, if not the best hole, on the course. You emerge from the dunes at the 15th, and play the finish over flatter fairways which parallel the closing holes on the Championship course. There are those who believe the shorter course to be the stiffer test of golf. Play both courses and judge for yourself.

KILKEEL
18 holes – par 72 (5921 metres/6579 yards)
3 miles from Kilkeel on the A2 to Warrenpoint.
Green Fees: £16 weekdays, £20 weekends and bank holidays.
Telephone: 028 417 65095/62296

The club was founded in 1922 but the present course is a more recent creation. It was laid out in the 1990s on 120 acres of woodland bought from the estate of the Earls of Kilmorey – the ancestors of the former Northern Ireland minister, Richard Needham. The layout was designed by Eddie Hackett assisted by the club's head greenkeeper, Jim Jones. Eleven new holes were cut through mature oak and beech woods and added to seven from the previous layout. The result is a wonderful parkland course with tree-lined fairways, lovely views of the sea and the Mountains of Mourne, a stream that comes into play on four holes and a pond which makes the 14th one of the most difficult and memorable on the course. It opens with an unusual par 5. The fairway is at a 90° angle to the tee. You drive through an avenue of tall trees to the fairway and turn left towards the well-defended green. The 2nd is uphill all the way – and you can't see the flag from the tee. The first views of the sea and the Mournes are from the cunningly bunkered 5th which climbs steeply to the green and begins a fine sequence of holes. At the 6th you must lay up before the stream that crosses the fairway or hope your second shot will hold the upward slope to the green and not roll back into the water. The 7th is a sharp dogleg left; the 8th a par 3 of classic simplicity – the hole slopes right and there's a big bunker left of the green. In late spring, the woodland in this corner of the course is filled with bluebells. Blue jays nest by the 9th fairway. The 13th (par 4) is classic golf-hole. Two large trees stand sentry on either side of the dogleg right. You need a perfect tee-shot up the left side to be able to see the green. The 14th is a dogleg left – with the added difficulty of the pond in front of the green. Enjoy the view of craggy Slieve Binnian (Sliabh Binneán – "Mountain of the Little Peak") on the 18th. With out-of-bounds on the left and the stream flowing across the fairway in front of the elevated green, it makes a fine finish. Jim Jones believes in keeping greens in play throughout the year – a task made easier by the micro-climate of the area. Kilkeel is the driest place in Ulster.

WARRENPOINT
18 holes – par 71 (5618metres/6242yards)
Lower Dromore Road, Warrenpoint.
Green Fees: £21 weekdays, £28 weekends and bank holidays.
Telephone: 028 41752371

If Warrenpoint's layout was lifted and dropped somewhere else in the Irish countryside it would be easier to appreciate its strengths. Traffic noise from the main road which runs along the perimeter of the course can be distracting. Although the sea is less than a 7-iron away, this is a parkland course. It's surrounded by roads and so cannot expand in any direction. All effort is therefore concentrated on keeping it in tip-top condition. The course is beautifully planted with trees and shrubs and has lovely views of the Carlingford mountains. Despite being a mere 88 acres – 120 acres is nowadays considered the minimum for 18 holes – it has plenty of variety. There are four par 5s and five par 3s. Hollows and

ridges, combined with strategic bunkering and judicious tree planting, demand thoughtful placing of the ball. For example, the 7th (par 4) has trees in front of the tee. You must go over them or go around them. The approach to the green is guarded by two big trees. On the 13th (par 4) the narrow fairway slopes towards out-of-bounds on the right and a ridge runs down the middle. In general, the difficulties are within 100 yards of the greens. You need a tidy short game to score well here – which may explain the large number of low handicaps among the members. Warrenpoint is the home club of Ronan Rafferty and Paddy Gribben.

BEYOND THE 18TH GREEN

The Mourne Mountains are enclosed by a circle of roads – the A2 from Newcastle to Rostrevor; the B25 from Rostrevor to Hilltown; the B8 from Hilltown to Castlewellan; and the A50 from Castlewellan to Newcastle. Only one road crosses the Mournes – the very scenic B27 from Kilkeel to Hilltown.

Newcastle (An Caisleán Nua "The New Castle") takes its name from a sixteenth-century castle which once stood where the River Shimna (Abhainn na Simhne – "River of the Bullrushes") flows into Dundrum Bay. Slieve Donard towers over the town. **Donard Park** has fine walks from its car park up to the Glen River which cascades down the mountain. The **Mourne Heritage Trust** on the Central Promenade organises weekend walks for visitors and provides information about the mountains. (Open Monday to Friday, 9am–5pm. Telephone: 028 437 24059) You can walk the length of the town along the promenade, passing the Percy French Memorial Fountain in the Promenade Gardens. An inscribed stone in the wall near a warm sea-water pool, commemorates the 1910 flight along the beach in a home-made mono-plane by Harry Ferguson, the inventor of the tractor.

North of **Newcastle** on A2 is the village of **Dundrum** (Dún Droma – "Fort of the Ridge") and **Dundrum Castle**. The thirteenth-century circular keep is just visible above the tall trees which surround the ruins on a rocky hill commanding views of sea and countryside for miles around. John de Courcy's original motte-and-bailey castle (c1177) was captured by King John in 1210, occupied by the Magennises in the fourteenth century, and sacked by Cromwell's troops in the seventeenth century. The keep, within the thirteenth-century upper ward has a spiral staircase and two latrines built into the curtain wall. In the basement of the keep is a funnel-shaped pit into which sub-soil water percolated.

The sand-hills that stretch along the coast from **Dundrum** to **Newcastle** form **Murlough National Nature Reserve** (Murlach – "Sea Inlet"). They have yielded relics dating from Neolithic to mediaeval times. (A particular shape of bowl with a heavy rim is called the Dundrum Bowl). The dune system merges into heathland and is inhabited by a wide range of plants, insects and birds. There is open access to the Nature Reserve all year round. The car park is clearly signposted from the A2 south of **Dundrum**. In summer, National Trust wardens lead guided walks through restricted areas of the dunes. (Details from The National Trust Interpretative Centre at the car park. Telephone: 028 437 51467)

The A2 south from Newcastle clings to the coast below the mountains. At the southern end of the town there is barely enough room for the road between the mountains and the sea. Two miles south of the town a sign welcomes you to the Kingdom of Mourne. Nearby is **Bloody Bridge** – so-called for a massacre here during the 1641 Rebellion. The coast from Newcastle to Greencastle was notorious for smuggling in the eighteenth and nineteenth centuries. Liquor, tobacco, tea, silk and soap were landed at deserted beaches and carried by packhorses through the mountains to Hilltown. The main smugglers' trail, known as the **Brandy Pad**, begins at Bloody Bridge.

At the fishing village of **Annalong** (Áth na Long – "The Ford of the Ships") below the jagged peak of Slieve Binnian, a restored corn mill at the deep-water harbour is powered by a waterwheel and produces flour and oatmeal. (Open February to November 11am–5pm except Sunday and Monday. Telephone: 028 437 68736)

The **Silent Valley** reservoir – opened in 1933 – was created by damming the Kilkeel river valley and took 30 years to build. Two dams were created below Slieve Binnian and Ben Crom. The catchment area was enclosed by the famous **Mourne Wall** – up to 8 feet high, 3 feet wide, and 22 miles long – connecting the summits of 15 mountains. A blaze of heather covers the valley sides in summer. You can walk three miles from the car park to the upper dam all year round. A shuttle bus operates daily during July and August and at weekends in May, June and September. It is a lovely spot. (Signposted from the A2. Reservoir grounds open daily 10am–6.30pm from May to September; 10am–4pm from October to April.)

The B27 from **Silent Valley** climbs past Pigeon Rock on the left and Slieve Muck (Sliabh Muc – "Mountain of Pigs") on the right to **Spelga Dam** – the highest road point in Ulster (Speilgeach – "Place of Pointed Rocks"). Turn left along the side of the dam and enjoy the spectacular views over the countryside below. (The next turning left off the B27 is a very pretty road down the mountains to **Rostrevor**.)

Greencastle (An Caisleán na hOireanaí – "Castle of the Cultivated Place") was the ancient capital of the Kingdom of Mourne. The castle – built by Henry III in 1252 – stands on a rocky outcrop about 300 yards from the shore guarding the entrance to Carlingford Lough. It was one of the English outposts in Ulster before the Elizabethan conquest and was twice destroyed by the Irish and rebuilt by the English. The ruins include a fourteenth-century keep, crenellated corner turrets and outworks.

Along the road to Greencastle the local council has erected signs with the names of the townlands through which you pass. A townland is a rural neighbourhood. There are 60,462 in Ireland and none is bigger than 300 acres. Thomas Colby (1784–1852), who carried out the first Ordnance Survey of Ireland in 1846, named them all, anglicising their Gaelic names. (His survey is the context for Brian Friel's play *Translations*.) People are still identified by the townland in which they live or from which they came. The Post Office long ago introduced postal codes to Northern Ireland, but country people are very proud of their townland names and still use them. It is so much nicer to say you live in, for example, Contifleece or Maddydrumbrisk, than at an anonymous number on the Belfast Road. The neat white houses at Greencastle pier were built for the lighthouse keepers. There are lovely views of Slieve Binnian and Carlingford Lough from here.

The A2 continues to **Rostrevor** (Ros Treabhair – "Trevor's Wood"). Because of its situation on the south-west slopes of the mountains where they roll down to **Carlingford Lough** it enjoys a warm micro-climate. Mediterranean plants like mimosa bloom in the gardens. The hillsides are a blaze of colour in early summer. The tall obelisk by the side of the road commemorates Major-General Robert Ross (1766–1814) who commanded a small British force which captured Washington in 1814 and burned the White House.

From the car park in **Rostrevor Forest**, walk the half-mile to the viewpoint, and see **Cloughmore** (An Cloch Mór – "The Great Stone") the enormous 40-tons boulder said to have been thrown from across **Carlingford Lough** by Finn MacCool. More prosaically, it was deposited by a glacier during the Ice Age which shaped the landscape of the Mournes.

The lough narrows at **Warrenpoint** (An Pointe – "The Point") and becomes like the fiords familiar to the Vikings who gave Carlingford Lough its name. **Narrow Water Castle** near the town was built in 1560 as an English garrison to guard the river estuary.

The B7 and B8 from **Warrenpoint** or the B25 from **Rostrevor** will take you to **Hilltown** on the upper reaches of the River Bann. The village takes its name not from its situation but from Wills Hill, first Marquis of Downshire, who built the Church of Ireland parish church of Saint John (1766). The town is an angling centre. Notice the weathervane on the cupola of the early nineteenth-century Downshire Arms Hotel – it's a fish. The many pubs in the town are a reminder of the **Brandy Pad** smuggling trail which ended here.

Continue east on the B8 and take a right turn onto the A25 to **Castlewellan**. On the left, **Drumena Cashel** (Drum Eanaigh – "Ridge of the Marsh") overlooks Lough Island Reavey. It dates from the early Christian period, has oval shaped dry-stone walls 10 feet thick and 6 feet high, and a souterrain which you can enter. Above ground are the remains of sixth- to tenth-century farmsteads.

Castlewellan like other villages in the Mournes was a stronghold of the Magennis family before they were dispossessed of their lands after the 1641 Rebellion. It owes its present layout around two tree-lined squares to William Annesley who became the local landlord in 1740. The Annesley estate was bought by the Forestry Service in 1967 and is now **Castlewellan Forest Park**. The **National Arboretum** was begun by the fourth Earl of Annesley who also built the Scottish baronial style castle (1856) now used as a conference centre. The **Arboretum** includes a walled garden beautifully sited on a south-facing hill. The garden, which has two huge wellingtonias at its entrance, is divided into themed walks. You can see the parent trees of the popular cypress "Castlewellan Gold" which was cultivated here. The tallest tree is a western hemlock with a self-sowed seedling underneath. They are known as "Mother and Child". The glasshouses have tropical birds and South American plants such as the Brazilian spider flower. There is a three-mile walk around the ornamental lake. In spring and early summer it reflects the camellias, rhododendrons and azaleas planted nearby. The wood between the lake and the castle is most beautiful in autumn. (Open all year round.)

The Forestry Service also runs **Tollymore Forest Park** – signposted on the road from **Castlewellan** to **Newcastle**. It was designed in the mid-eighteenth century for the first Earl of Clanbrassil by the garden architect Thomas Wright. He favoured the informal "gothick" style then in fashion. The entrance to the estate is a barbican gate. A barn is disguised as a gothic church. There are forest walks with fine views and a riverside walk with bridges across the Shimna and Spinkwee rivers, an obelisk and a grotto. (Open all year 10am–dusk.)

TOURIST INFORMATION

Newcastle Tourist Information Centre: 10-14 Central Promenade, Newcastle Co. Down   BT33 0AA
Telephone: 028 437 22222
Warrenpoint Tourist Information Centre: The Town Hall, Church Street, Warrenpoint
Telephone: 028 417 52256

Opposite page:
Castlewellan Forest Park

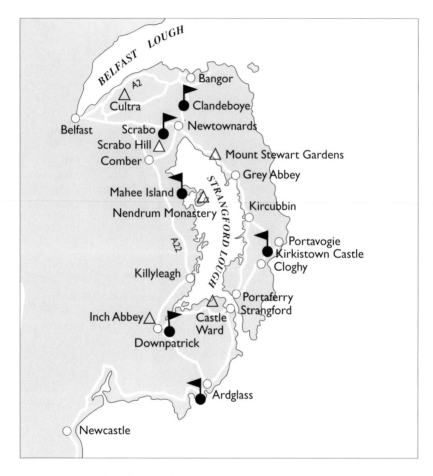

(Golf Courses: Clandeboye, Kirkistown, Ardglass, Downpatrick, Mahee Island and Scrabo.)

Distances: Belfast to Newtownards 10km/6miles; Newtownards to Portaferry 30km/19miles; Newtownards to Downpatrick 34km/21miles; Downpatrick to Ardglass 10km/6miles.

Strangford is Ireland's largest sea lough, and has the narrowest entrance. The scenery changes with the tides. When the tide is out you can see oyster-catchers, redshanks and curlews on the mudflats which stretch far out into the lough. When the tide is in, the lough looks like a freshwater lake. Glaciation formed much of the landscape here. The low rounded hills characteristic of County Down are known as "drumlins". The word is peculiar to this part of the world and is derived from "droim" (a ridge). Drumlins surface as small islands in the lough where sea birds nest and breed.

The Vikings named the lough Strangrfjorthr – "Strong Sea Inlet" – because of the swirling currents at its narrow entrance. In AD432, Saint Patrick, sailing north along the Irish coast, was swept off-course and through the tidal narrows to make landfall near Downpatrick. The gothic outline of **Scrabo Tower**, built on Scrabo Hill, 152metres/500ft above sea level, dominates the landscape for miles around the busy market town of **Newtownards** (Baile Nua na hArda – "New Town of the Promontory") at the northern end of the lough. The peninsula which runs south from here is 37km/23 miles long and never more than 8km/5miles wide. A five-minute journey by car ferry takes you from its southern tip at **Portaferry** (Port an Pheire – "Landing-place of the Ferry") to where Saint Patrick landed more than 1,500 years ago. You can make a complete tour of the lough beginning and ending at any point on the route.

CLANDEBOYE

Dufferin 18 holes – par 71 (5993metres/6559yards)
Ava 18 holes – par 70 (5258metres/5755yards)
Above the village of Conlig off the A21 between Bangor and Newtownards.
Green Fees: Dufferin £27.50 weekdays, £33 weekends;
Ava £22 weekdays, £27 weekends.
Telephone: 028 91 271767

Clandeboye golf club is not well signposted – but well worth finding. Follow signs for Conlig (An Chonleac "The Houndstone") and look for the signpost in the middle of the village. As you drive up the hill and into the visitors' car park, the first thing you notice is the splendid clubhouse which looks out over Belfast Lough. The second thing you notice is the warm welcome. After that you have to decide whether to play the Dufferin or the Ava. Both courses took their present shape in the early 1970s. The first Clandeboye course was created in 1933 on the former estate of the Marquis of Dufferin and Ava. He named his house and estate Clandeboye (Clann Aodha Bui – "The Family of Yellow-haired Hugh") after one of the Tyrone O'Neill's who settled here in the thirteenth century, hence the club's name. In the 1970s this course was divided. Nine holes were added to the original first nine to make the championship length Dufferin. The back nine became the basis of what is now the Ava. Perhaps the German architect, Baron von Limburger, who designed the present layout had in mind the old German saying: "he who has the choice has the agony". What you have at Clandeboye is an agonising choice between the charm of the Ava and the splendour of the Dufferin. The latter loops twice around a ring-fort crowned with trees. On the 1st tee you face a daunting drive over thickets of gorse to the fairway which slopes downhill and left. On a clear day you can see Ailsa Craig from here. The Ava has an uphill start and a great par 5 second with out-of-bounds all the way up the left-hand side. There are fine views of Strangford Lough, woods with bluebells, and thickets of gorse. On the Dufferin, look out for the ancient standing stone between the 16th green and the 17th tee. Long hitters might prefer the Dufferin but the Ava is great fun.

KIRKISTOWN CASTLE
18 holes – par 69 (5616metres/6146yards)
In the village of Cloughey on the A2 to Portaferry.
Green Fees: £15 weekdays, £20 weekends.
Telephone: 028 42 771233

"If only this spot were within 50 miles of London!" said James Braid (designer of Gleneagles) when he extended the links at Kirkistown in 1929. Although no longer wholly a links course, Kirkistown's proud boast is "we never close". Well, hardly ever. Perhaps a half-day in a whole year. The greenkeepers' difficulties are with larks and historic monuments. Sometimes the rough can't be cut because of larks nesting. They stroll around the 7th and sing as they fly above the course. The gorse-covered Norman motte which catches the errant approach shot to the 10th green is an ancient burial ground and listed monument. The ruined tower at the elevated green on the terrific 2nd hole was the lookout tower for Kirkistown Castle which adjoins the course and comes into view on several holes. It was built in 1622 by the Savage family who were Norman landlords in Ards. On a clear day you can see the Isle of Man and Scotland. The wind is always a factor. Sometimes a light breeze, sometimes blowing so strongly it lifts the flags out of the holes! To play here on a windy day is an exhilarating experience and a true test of golf. Among recent changes to Braid's design are extra bunkers – for example on the 5th and 12th – to catch today's longer hitters. (NB the tee beside the 11th green is the 14th.) The 12th is played up towards the castle. The 17th is played from an elevated tee with fine sea views out over dense gorse which tumbles to the fairway below. A well-judged tee shot on the 18th will avoid the gullies to the left and right of the fairway and take you safely back to the clubhouse.

ARDGLASS
18 holes – par 70 (5498metres/6017yards)
Beside the harbour in Ardglass – 7 miles from Downpatrick on the B1.
Green Fees: £18 weekdays, £24 weekends.
Telephone: 028 44 841219

Ardglass Golf Course

The first five holes take you up on to the cliffs along the rocky shoreline. From every part of the course you can see the Mountains of Mourne sweep down to the sea. Unless, of course, it's raining and the Mournes are hidden by the clouds. It happens sometimes; but Ardglass is largely a links course and drains well. Your head gets wet but your feet stay dry. When the weather is fine you can see not only Slieve Donard (Sliabh Donairt – "St Donart's Mountain") the highest mountain in Ulster, but also Slieve Croob (Sliabh Cruibe – "Mountain of the Hoof") the source of the River Lagan. It lies north of the Mournes, further inland. You can even see the Isle of Man. Curlews cry overhead, oyster-catchers bank and dive, fishing boats head in and out of the harbour. This is a memorable course of great character. The 2nd is played over a rocky inlet to a plateau green. The 6th is uphill and over a dry-stone wall. The 9th green is beside a traditional whitewashed cottage. The 11th is played from an elevated tee overlooking Coney Island – made famous by a Van Morrison song. The 18th brings you back down to the clubhouse – built on fourteenth-century foundations. Play the course in autumn and winter and return to a roaring fire and a hot whiskey in the clubhouse. Play on a fine day in summer and think yourself in heaven.

DOWNPATRICK
18 holes – par 70 (5574metres/6100yards)
On the Saul Road out of Downpatrick, about 1.5 miles from the town.
Green Fees: £15 weekdays, £20 weekends, £7 winter.
Telephone: 028 4461 5947

This is a very pleasant parkland course laid out on high ground above the town of Downpatrick with views of the Mountains of Mourne, the Dromara Hills and

Strangford Lough to divert the eye from encroaching housing estates. The light loamy turf is springy and dry underfoot. The course dries out quickly after rain and is often open for play when other parkland courses are waterlogged. It's lightly bunkered but the greens are not large. This is a design which relies on the lie of the land and judicious tree planting for its difficulties. Natural ridges cross several fairways and are a marked feature of the course. On the 5th hole (a long par 4 for men, par 5 for ladies) you want to open your shoulders and strike towards Strangford Lough in the far distance but only a very long hitter will clear the two grassy mounds on the middle of the fairway which falls steeply to the green. The 7th (par 4 for men, par 5 for ladies) is a lovely challenge. The fairway curves gently downhill and to the right with the boundary hedge on the right and two large trees in the middle of the fairway. The 11th is a very pretty par 3 defended by a pond, a bunker and a large and graceful tree. The 18th fairway slopes slightly left and the green is to the left through a narrow gap in trees. A strong finish.

MAHEE ISLAND
9 holes – par 68 (5108metres/5588yards)
From Comber take the Killyleagh Road and turn left at first signpost to Ardmillan. Then bear left for 6 miles to Mahee Island.
Green Fees: £10 weekdays, £15 weekends and bank holidays.
Telephone: 028 97 541234

Mahee Island golf course is signposted from the Comber to Killyleagh Road. If you come at it from any other direction you are likely to lose your way in a maze of small roads which rise and fall gently over drumlins and give tantalising glimpses of the lough and its myriad islands. It's a very pretty area to get lost in. Mahee Island is reached by a causeway from another island. You are almost completely surrounded by water. From the first tee you look out over other low islands dotted about the lough. The hazards are nearly all in the lie of the land – except on the 8th/17th (par 3) which requires a short downhill shot to a well-bunkered, contoured green. The first fairway falls steeply right to the water's edge. The 2nd/11th (par 4) runs up along a boundary hedge to a small green. Overhit on the 4th/13th (par 3) and you're in the water. The 7th/16th is played along the side of the hill. The 9th/18th is a dogleg around the hill. Fred Daly, who won the British Open in 1947, was the club's first professional and greenkeeper in the early 1930s. This is where he perfected the cut-up, lofted shot for which he was famous. "I could pop ball after ball into a hole halfway up one of the trees on the course," he said. Mahee Island is exceptionally tidy with plentiful well-disguised litter-bins and a clearly designated area for cleaning shoes and trolleys before leaving the course.

SCRABO
18 holes – par 71 (5722metres/6262yards)
From Newtownards, follow signs for Scrabo Country Park.

Green Fees: £15 Monday–Saturday, £20 Sunday.
Telephone: 028 91 812355

Scrabo Tower – built in 1857 as a memorial to the third Marquis of Londonderry – is one of the best known landmarks in Northern Ireland. It sits on an outcrop of basalt high above the northern reaches of the lough, and its tall, brooding gothic outline can be seen for miles around. On spring bank holidays and in the summer, you can climb 122 steps to the top and look down on the golf course on the high plateau below – surely one of the most extraordinary sights in Ireland. This course needs no bunkers. Gorse abounds. Mounds of it. Clumps of it. Valleys filled with it. Besides the whins, there are rocky outcrops and rabbit holes. On several fairways there are large, evenly spaced undulations which look like giant potato drills. Which is what they were during the Second World War when golf courses were requisitioned for food production. The first hole gives immediate indication of the difficulties ahead. It's stroke index one for men and requires a mighty strike uphill to a green surrounded, naturally, by gorse. The 3rd fairway, a slight dogleg left, crosses the first fairway and is filled with bumps and hollows like a links. The 12th requires a long hit over rocks and heather to a fairway which bends right and uphill. The whole course slopes away from the tower and the land drops away steeply from the edge of the course and the plateau. The 16th has a blind approach up and over a rocky cliff to the green. On the 17th tee, birds bank and wheel below you to your right as you flight the ball over tumbling whins to the green about 80 feet below in a rocky gorse-lined enclosure. This is one of the most idiosyncratic golf courses you are likely to encounter. Unforgettable.

BEYOND THE 18TH GREEN

The A20 south from **Newtownards** hugs the shoreline of the lough and after about 8 miles passes the National Trust house and gardens at **Mount Stewart**. This was the home of Robert Stewart, Lord Castlereagh (1769–1822) British foreign secretary during the Napoleonic wars. The house displays objects associated with his career – such as the 22 Empire chairs used by the delegates at the Congress of Vienna in 1815. The gardens are the most celebrated in Ulster. They were created by Edith, Lady Londonderry who combined plants from every continent to make a garden of great quality and character. She surrounded the house with an intricate series of gardens, creating formal and informal vistas. Stone figures of dodos, dinosaurs, griffins and other mythological creatures dot the terraces. There are Italian, Spanish, English and Irish gardens. Irish emblems are cut in topiary. The Red Hand of Ulster is patterned in the paving. Paths from the gardens wind into woodland around a lake. The eighteenth-century neoclassical "Temple of the Winds" designed for eating al fresco, stands on a wooded hillside. It has a spiral staircase and splendid views over Strangford Lough. (Open March to October. Telephone: 028 42 788387.)

Still hugging the coastline, the A20 takes you next to **Greyabbey** (An Mhainis tir Liath –"The Grey Monastery"). The town takes its name from the twelfth-century Cistercian abbey founded here by Affreca, daughter of the King of Man and wife of the Norman baron, John de Courcy. The abbey ruins, in sheltered grounds with lawns and gardens, include triple lancet windows and a fine west door.

The A20 continues south to the fishing and boating village of Kircubbin (Cill Ghobáin – "Goban's Church") named for an early Christian church which once stood to the east of the village. You can gather mussels and cockles on the rocky shore. **Portaferry** is on "the Narrows" at the entrance to the lough. This is a centre for sea and lough fishing and yachting. Five defensive tower houses were built to guard it. The lough is home to over 2,000 species of marine life from sea anemones to sponges. You can see them in the Northern Ireland aquarium close to the ruined tower house which is a prominent feature in the town.

There's never very long to wait for the car ferry to the village of **Strangford** on the opposite west side of the narrows. From the deck of the ferry there are lovely views of the lough. You get an idea of its strategic importance from the five small castles and five towers. From the harbour take the A25 to **Downpatrick**. After 2 km there's a sign to **Castleward** National Trust property.

Castleward house, built in 1762, is a domestic compromise. Bernard Ward, the first Lord Bangor, favoured classical architecture. His wife, Lady Anne, preferred the Strawberry Hill Gothic, made fashionable by Horace Walpole. They split the difference. The front of the house – facade and interior – is neoclassical. The back of the house, overlooking the gardens and the lough, is elaborately neo-Gothic. The front reception rooms have Doric columns and graceful panelling. Her Ladyship's rooms have quatrefoils, pointed doorways and fan vaulting. The landscaped grounds and sunken garden are charming. Lady Anne's Temple – a Palladian folly – overlooks Temple Water, created in the eighteenth century to reflect the temple and the picturesque ruins of Audley Castle in the grounds. There is a **Castleward Opera Festival** in June. The grounds are open all year. The house is open from March to October. (Telephone: 028 44 881204.)

The A25 brings you next to **Downpatrick** (Dún Pádraig – "Patrick's Fort") the county town. The area around Downpatrick is known as **Lecale**. The town was built on an ancient hill fort where Saint Malachy in the sixth century founded a church and monastery dedicated to Saint Patrick. The Book of Armagh (AD802) in Trinity College Dublin, records the burial of Saint Patrick on this hill. An adjoining drumlin (known locally as "The Mound") where the Quoile and Blackstaff rivers flow into Strangford Lough, bears traces of pre-Christian settlement.

Nendrum Monastic Site, Mahee Island

The Anglo-Norman John de Courcy made Downpatrick his capital, and brought over Benedictine monks from Chester. In 1316 the abbey was destroyed by Edward Bruce of Scotland. The rebuilt abbey – finished in 1512 – was again destroyed in the Elizabethan conquest. The ruins of the choir and fragments of stone carvings remained and were incorporated into the nineteenth-century reconstruction which stands today. The unique box pews are characteristic of the Regency period. The original Norman font was rescued from a local farmyard. (The cathedral is open to visitors 10am–5pm Monday to Saturday and 2pm–5pm on Sunday.)

Street names in Downpatrick reflect the pattern of settlement in Ireland – Irish Street, English Street and Scotch Street. **Down County Museum** in English Street, is a former military barracks and jail. Thomas Russell, a leader of two rebellions in 1798 and 1803 was hanged at the entrance gate. You can visit the cell blocks where convicts were held before transportation to Australia. A section of the museum is devoted to Saint Patrick and the area's role in the early Christian Church.

At **Saul** (Sabhall – "Barn") two miles from the town (just past Downpatrick golf course) the Church of Ireland built a small church on the site of the barn in which Saint Patrick first said Mass in Ireland in AD432. He died at Saul in AD461. (The church is open every day 9am–5pm.)

At **Struell Wells** (An tSruthail – "The Stream") in a secluded rocky valley about a mile from the town on the B1 road to **Ardglass**, are two holy wells and the ruins of two mediaeval bath houses along the course of an icy underground stream. The smaller, roofless building by a sycamore tree was the women's house. The larger, barrel-vaulted and slated bath house was for men. The buildings are by a small grassy area in the middle of which is the eye well. Water flows from a drinking well, through the eye well to the bath houses. (Visit anytime.)

Ardglass (Ard Ghlas – "Green Height") as its name suggests is built on a hill above a deep harbour. The fifteenth-century **Jordan's Castle** in the middle of the town was one of a series of fortified towers and warehouses built to protect the port.

North of the town, the ruins of **Inch Abbey** (Inis Chumhscraigh) occupy a peaceful site by the Quoile River. The abbey was destroyed by Vikings in 1001 and rebuilt by John de Courcy in 1180. The east end of this latter building with three late Romanesque lancet windows (*c*1200) survives. The entire foundations have been excavated and include a fifteenth-century well and bake-house. (Visit anytime.)

From Downpatrick the A22 takes you along the western shore of Strangford Lough to **Killyleagh** (Cill O Laoch – "Church of Laoch") a plantation town formally arranged in a grid pattern. The hilltop castle dates from the fourteenth century. It was restored in 1666 and again in the 1850s when the architect Sir Charles Lanyon added the turrets and crenellations which rise above the town like a castle in Bavaria. Open air concerts are held in the grounds in summer. Sir Hans Sloane (1660–1753) founder of the British Museum, was born in Killyleagh. He settled in Chelsea in 1712 and is commemorated there in Sloane Square and Hans Place.

A right turn at **Balloo Cross Road**s on the A22 leads down to **Whiterock** and **Sketrick Island** (Skothryggr – "Humpback Ridge" in Old Norse) and winds north along the shore to **Nendrum Monastery** (Naoindroim – "Nine Drumlins") and **Mahee Island** (Inis Mochaoi – "Mochao's Island"). **Nendrum** is one of the best excavated early Christian sites in Ireland and is beautifully situated on a hill at the junction of two islands in the lough beside the entrance to Mahee Island golf club. Saint Mochaoi, who was converted to Christianity by Saint Patrick, is said to have founded the monastery in the early fifth century although archaeological evidence points to c700. This is one of the quietest and most atmospheric early Christian sites. From the roadside gate you climb the small hill to the ruined settlement. It's enclosed by three concentric stone walls (cashels) which circle the hill. Inside the enclosure are the base of a round tower, a ruined church with an unusual sundial and a graveyard. A small museum describes daily life in an early mediaeval Irish monastery. (Site always open.

Museum open April to September. Tuesday–Saturday 10–6pm. Sundays 2–6pm. Telephone: 028 91 874146.)

Brent geese, shelducks, wigeons and whooper swans are among the winter visitors to Strangford Lough. About 75% of the world's total population of brent geese winter and breed here. (A festival is held every year to celebrate their arrival.) Arctic, common, sandwich and roseate terns are summer visitors. At **Castle Espie** on the road from **Mahee Island** to **Comber** you can view Ireland's largest collection of waterfowl from specially constructed hides in the **Wildfowl And Wetlands Trust gardens**. (Open all year. Telephone: 028 91 874146.)

Newtownards was founded during the Protestant Plantation of Ulster in the early seventeenth-century by a Scotsman called Hugh Montgomery. The ruins of a thirteenth-century Dominican priory – founded by the Savage family – stand in Court Square. The monastery was suppressed by Henry VIII in 1541. Hugh, first Viscount Montgomery, rebuilt the north aisle and added the entrance tower which bears his initials. The market cross in the High Street dates from 1635. The Londonderry family succeeded the Montgomerys as landlords of Newtownards. **Scrabo Tower**, on the plateau above the town, was built to commemorate the third Marquis of Londonderry. It stands in **Scrabo Country Park** (signposted from the town). The views from the tower are stupendous. (Tower open at Easter, May bank holidays and June to September daily, 10.30am–6pm.)

The Folk Park at the **Ulster Folk And Transport Museum** at **Cultra** (Baile Chúl Trá – "Townland at the back of the Strand") has whole houses and terraces removed stone by stone from towns and countryside and re-erected in a setting as close as possible to the landscape in which they were originally built. A guide in each building explains its history and usage. There are cottages and farmhouses, a flax mill, a blacksmith's forge, and other relics of rural industry. Demonstrations of horse-ploughing, wheat threshing, and other traditional farming methods go on all year. The transport section features the Irish Railway Collection and the De Lorean sports car, as well as boats and planes.

TOURIST INFORMATION

Downpatrick Tourist Information Centre: 74 Market Street,
Downpatrick, Co. Down BT33 6LZ
Telephone: 028 44 612233.

Newtownards Tourist Information Centre: 31 Regent Street,
Newtownards BT23 4AD
Telephone: 028 91 826846.

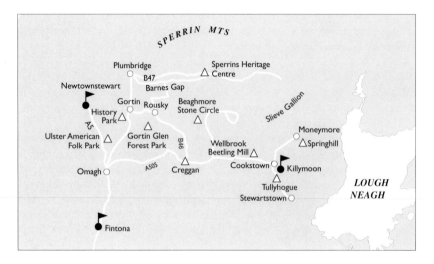

(Golf Courses: Killymoon, Newtownstewart and Fintona)

Distances: Cookstown to Omagh 40km/25miles; Omagh to Newtownstewart 16km/10miles; Omagh to Fintona 12km/7.5miles; Omagh to Gortin 15km/9.5miles.

County Tyrone is one of the loveliest and least known counties in Ireland. It's aptly called "Tyrone among the bushes". Gorse, heather, hawthorn, holly, hazel, birch and rowan adorn the hedgerows, line the rivers and fill the glens. Tyrone stretches from the west shores of Lough Neagh (the largest lake in the British Isles) to the edge of the Donegal Mountains. The landscape is always gentle – from the rich, rolling hills of south Tyrone, to the higher, lonelier, brown and gold slopes of the Sperrin Mountains in the north of the county. Tyrone is full of hidden treasures, like the golf courses at Killymoon, Newtownstewart and Fintona. You can even pan for gold in the Sperrin mountain streams.

KILLYMOON
18 holes – par 70 (5496metres/6015yards)
Cookstown. Signposted at the south end of the town.

Killymoon Golf Course

Green Fees: £10 Monday, £18 Tuesday to Friday, £22 weekends.
Telephone: 028 867 63762

At £10 for 18 holes on a Monday, Killymoon is a terrific bargain for the visiting golfer. This pleasing parkland course, on land that once belonged to nearby Killymoon Castle, holds an honoured place in the history of Irish golf. It was founded in 1890, and one year later was a founder member of the Golfing Union of Ireland. Rhona Adair, daughter of Killymoon's founder – Hugh Adair – was a golfing sensation a century ago. She first competed in the Ladies' British Open Amateur Championship in 1895 – aged 13. She won the title in 1900 and 1903. And she won the Irish Women's Championship in four successive years from 1900 to 1903. Killymoon is a compact, parkland course with lovely views of Slieve Gallion and the softly rolling farmland of Tyrone. Club tradition says you can see all the other five counties of Northern Ireland from the top of the hill on the 9th. (It also says the longest drive was a slice at the 6th that landed the ball on a train travelling parallel to the fairway and took it all the way to Stewartstown.) Trains no longer run on this line, but the grassy track can still be seen alongside the 6th and 7th holes. Unusually, there are two par 3s in succession on the opening nine. The 7th is a challenging drive from an elevated tee to a slightly raised green defended by two well-placed bunkers that force an approach from the right. The 8th is uphill through an avenue of trees to an elevated green. The 9th is a difficult par 4 with a blind tee-shot over the hill from which you have the most extensive views on the course. The road to the castle runs behind the green and is not out-of-bounds. Four holes are now played on the other side of this quiet road. (Members call this part of the course "The Garden of Eden". If you have so far been recording a good score, these next four holes could cause you to fall from grace.) The 10th (par 4) calls for a blind drive towards a distant gap in the trees. The fairway then slopes down towards the castle (out of sight) and the very pretty green surrounded by trees and shrubs. The 11th (par 3) has a very difficult, contoured green on three levels. The 12th takes you back up to the road. (The screeching you can hear is from the peacocks at the castle.) The road behind the 12th green is out-of-bounds this time. The 14th – back across the road on the main part of the course – is a lovely, long, par 5 that invites your drive. The road, on your left, is again out-of-bounds. Killymoon finishes with another blind tee-shot, and a second (you hope) to the green in front of the clubhouse. The turf at Killymoon seems to have a spring in it, and the greens can't be faulted.

NEWTOWNSTEWART

18 holes – par 70 (5341metres/5934yards)
2 miles southwest of Newtownstewart. (Signposted from the A5.)
Green Fees: £12 weekdays, £17 weekends and bank holidays.
Telephone: 028 81 662242

The wooded slopes of Bessie Bell and Mary Gray, in the foothills of the Sperrins, overlook this lovely, tree-lined course on land leased from the Duke of Abercorn's estate at Baronscourt. (Bessie Bell and Mary Gray are named after a Scottish ballad about "two bonnie lasses".) The stream that bisects the course is a tributary of the River Strule. But water comes into play only on the 4th (par 4) – The Sheugh – the first really testing hole. (As you walk to the 4th tee, check the pin position on the 6th green, to your right.) Before you lies a pretty, curved stone bridge over the sheugh (stream and ditch). You drive over a black and white marker stick on a hill that slopes steeply left into the sheugh. Over the hill, on the fairway, there is the unusual sight of a bunker, guarding the green at the bottom. Bunkers were only introduced at Newtownstewart in the last ten years. In general, the course relies on trees and slopes to create difficulty. Trees are a definite danger on the 5th – a sharp dogleg right – and on the 6th (par 5 for ladies) where the fairway falls away left into Baronscourt Forest. The tiered, plateau green is very hard to hold. The 8th is a difficult par 4 for men. The drive is over a hill. Dense trees line the left-hand side of the fairway, which then descends like a wide staircase to the green. (Ladies drive from the top of the hill.) You walk through woods, over the cascading stream; its steep banks lined with bluebells, primroses, wild garlic and celandines in spring, to the 9th tee. This part of the course is particularly peaceful. (Don't be surprised to see pheasants strolling across the fairways.) From the 10th tee (par 3) there are extensive views over the forest and the gentle, rolling countryside beyond. Knockavoe (Cnoc an Bhadhbha –"Hill of the Crow") Mountain is on your left. The 13th is a memorable pitch hole, downhill. The 14th is a long, uphill, par 5. You will be grateful for the short 15th (par 3) before embarking on another par 5 along the forest boundary. This has the trickiest green on the course. It slopes both left and right and a less than perfect putt can send your ball rolling right down the 17th fairway, or left into a hollow. You walk back through the woods and over the stream again for the closing hole.

FINTONA
9 holes – par 72 (5766metres/6406yards)
Entrance near the bridge in Fintona.
Green Fees: £10 weekdays before 2pm, £15 weekends, bank holidays and weekdays after 2pm.
Telephone: 028 82 841480

Fintona golf club lies in the grounds of the Ecclesville Desmesne on the edge of the town. The splendid clubhouse overlooks Quiggery Waters – the trout stream that flows through the course and curves around the 9th/18th green, at the bottom of a hill. (The weathervane on the clubhouse is a golfer – a nice touch.) The riverbank is beautifully terraced with big blocks of local stone (the first blastings from nearby Drumquin quarry). This striking water-feature was created by the brothers who keep the course in pristine condition – head greenkeeper Kevin McConnell and his assistant (and twin) Patrick McConnell. The round begins with a walk over a pretty wooden bridge to the 1st tee near a large, spreading beech tree. The green on this par 4 is straight ahead. The river is out-of-bounds on your left. It turns sharply right and crosses the fairway directly under the edge of the green. The beautiful, loud and varied birdsong, coming from the bushes and shrubbery by the 2nd tee, may distract you as you flight your ball to the undulating fairway, curving gently right towards the (unseen) green. The dense, woodland boundary of the course is on your left. On the right, the McConnell brothers have planted native trees – beech, oak, ash, elms, limes and chestnuts. The brown waters of the Quiggery flow through the woodland that runs down the middle of the course. The river comes into play again along the left-hand side of the 3rd fairway. (You may see a boy and his sheepdog rounding up lost balls.) The 4th is a par 3 over the river and its terraced stone bank. Then you walk up through a stand of trees for three holes played along the gentle slope of the hill. From here you glimpse the pretty church tower and steeple of St Lawrence's Church through the trees. There are different tee positions for the front and back nines. The 15th (par 4) for example, is 74metres/81yards longer than the 6th for men. The ladies play this hole as a par 4 on the front nine and a par 5 coming back, when the tee position makes it 125metres/137yards longer. The 8th is a par 3 played from an elevated tee across a dip to the green on the highest part of the course. From here you have lovely views over the town and lake with the Sperrin Mountains in the distance, and, to your right, the slopes of Fivemiletown Mountain – a patchwork of small fields, dotted with farms. The 9th/18th is a great downhill drive towards the river and the green on the opposite bank. Look out for red squirrels in the woods.

BEYOND THE 18TH GREEN

Fintona (Fionntamhnach – "Bright Clearing") was a centre for the linen industry in the eighteenth century and was once famous for its horse-drawn tram. It is the birthplace of the poet John Montague. (County Tyrone is also the birthplace of the playwright Brian Friel, the poet Alice Milligan, the novelist Flann O'Brien, the songwriter Jimmy Kennedy and ballad writer William Marshall.) The **Ecclesville Centre**, near the golf course, is a riding school and fitness centre run by the community. (Telephone: 028 82 840591)

The **Ulster American Folk Park** (signposted on the A5 from **Omagh**) tells the inter-related history of Ulster and the United States in the eighteenth and nineteenth centuries. You can use the database at the **Centre of Emigration Studies** to trace ancestors who emigrated to the US and Canada. Emigration from Ireland to North America was in two major phases. The first, in the eighteenth and early nineteenth centuries was by predominantly Presbyterian pioneers who had settled in Ulster during the Plantation. These early emigrants are known as the Scotch-Irish. The second phase was prompted by the famine of the 1840s. **Judge Thomas Mellon**, who founded a vast industrial empire, was only five years old when he emigrated from County Tyrone with his parents in 1818, but his childhood memories of Tyrone remained vivid all his life. His boyhood home is the centrepiece of the **Ulster American Folk Park** in which cabins, houses, schools, churches and shops have been moved piece by piece from their original sites in Ulster and America, and rebuilt around the **Mellon Homestead**, which stands on its original site. A route through the **Folk Park**, set in natural woodland of hawthorn, rowan, holly and birch, traces the emigrant experience from the Old World to the New – leaving the shops and dwellings of Ulster, passing through a recreated dockside and emigrant ship, and emerging in a New World town on the other side of the park. Guides in the costume of the era explain the background to each building. Craftsmen, like the blacksmith in the early nineteenth-century forge, demonstrate eighteenth- and nineteenth-century skills from Ulster and the United States. A tour through the park is absorbing, moving and not to be missed. (Open April to September 10.30am–4.30pm Monday to Saturday, 11am–5pm Sundays and bank holidays; October–April Monday to Friday 10.30am–5pm. Telephone: 028 8224 3292)

Omagh – (Ómaigh – "Sacred Plain") sits on a hill above the **Drumragh** (Droim Rátha – "Ridge of the Fort") and **Camowen** (Camabhainn – "Crooked River")

Beaghmore Stone Circle

rivers, which meet at the foot of the town to form the **River Strule** (Sruthail – "Stream"). The town and community were deeply scarred by the bomb that killed 29 people and injured hundreds on 15th August 1998. Omagh District Council is one of the most enterprising in Northern Ireland, promoting tourism through projects like the **History Park** in **Gortin**. You can follow a 5km/3mile signposted walk ("Highway to Health") from the car park near the bus station, around the town and along the river.

Newtownstewart is named for the Stewart family who acquired land forfeited by the O'Neills in the Plantation of Ulster in the early seventeenth century. The twin towers of the ruined fourteenth-century castle of the Irish chieftain Henry Aimbreidh O'Neill – **Harry Avery's Castle** – stand on a hill near the town (signposted). In the town's main street you can see the wall of the Stewart castle James II burned on his way back from his unsuccessful siege of Derry in 1688.

Cappagh Burn (Ceapach – "Tillage Plot") flows through the **Ulster History Park** and divides the townland of Cullion (Cuilleann – "Slope") from Lislap (Lios Leapa – "Fort of the Grave") between **Omagh** and **Gortin** (An Goirtín – "The Little Field"). Full-scale replicas – from the huts of the first hunter-gatherers 9,000 years ago, to the fortified manor house, cottage and mill of the Scottish and English planters – show how people in Ulster lived, worshipped and buried their dead from the Stone Age to the seventeenth century. A local craftsman, Michael Muldoon, copied the furniture in the fortified manor – hanging cupboard, dresser, four-poster, tables and chairs – from paintings of seventeenth-century interiors. Forestry pines are gradually being replaced by native trees – hazel, birch, alder, rowan, oak, ash and beech – to re-create the Tyrone landscape of the past. (Open daily 10am–6pm July and August; 10am–5.30pm April to June, and September; open weekdays 10am–5pm December to March. Telephone: 028 81648188)

The **Gortin Lakes Scenic Route** through **Boorin Nature Reserve** at **Gortin Forest Park** takes you past small lakes known as "kettle-holes" formed by glaciation, and gives a fine view over the valley of the **Owenkillew River** (Abhainn Choilleadh – "River of the Wood") and **Gortin**.

A small mountain road, signposted **Barnes Gap** (Bearnas – "Gap") will take you from the B46 to the **Glenelly Valley** (Gleann Aichle – "Glen of the Look-out") and the **Sperrins Heritage Centre** where you can learn about the geology of the **Sperrins** (Speirín – "Spur of Rock") and pan for gold in the nearby stream. (Open April to October 11.30am–6pm Monday to Saturday, 2pm–6pm Sundays. Telephone: 028 8164 8142)

An Creagán Visitor Centre, at the junction of the B46 and the A505 to **Cookstown** features displays about the cultural traditions of **Creggan** (An Creagán – "Stony Place"), the natural environment and the archaeology. (Open daily April to September 11am–6.30pm, weekdays only October to March 11am–4.30pm. Telephone: 028 8076 1112) You can rent bicycles and cycle 22km/14miles to **Beaghmore Stone Circle**. (This is the longest of five cycle routes to points of interest mapped by the visitor centre.)

The circles, lines and cairns at **Beaghmore** (An Bheitheach Mhór – "Place of Birches") were discovered during turf cutting in the early 1940s. There are hundreds of stones in rows leading to cairns, and seven circles – six of them paired. Charcoal from a hearth found near one of the cairns was dated to c2800BC. This may have been one of the earliest sites of human settlement in Ireland. The site is signposted from the A505. (Always open)

Wellbrook Beetling Mill on the banks of the **Ballinderry River** (Baile an Doire – "Townland of the Oak Wood") began linen beetling in 1764. The linen industry was brought to Ireland by French Huguenots. Linen is produced from flax, which grows well in the Irish climate. Bundles of flax were soaked, and then "scutched" to separate the fibres, which were then spun and woven. Bleached linen was smoothed by the "beetle hammers" you can see working at **Wellbrook**. The National Trust keeps the water-powered machinery in full working order. (Open weekends and bank holidays June to September 2pm–6pm. Open daily, except Tuesdays, July and August 2pm–6pm. Telephone: 028 8675 1735 or 028 8674 8210)

Slieve Gallion (Slieve gCallann – "Mountain of the Heights") dominates the landscape around **Cookstown** (An Chorr Chríochach – "The Boundary Hill"). The town is named after the planter Alan Cook who founded a settlement here in 1609. In 1628 he got a patent for the market that is still held in the town every Saturday when the main streets are filled with stalls. The design of the town owes most to William Stewart of **Killymoon** and is famous for its length (2km/1.25miles) and width. (The main streets are said to be as wide as O'Connell Street in Dublin.) In 1803 William Stewart employed the famous architect **John Nash** to design **Killymoon Castle** (not open to the public) and the very beautiful **Derryloran Church** (C of I) at the southern end of the town.

From the eleventh to the sixteenth century, the O'Neill kings of Ulster were crowned and anointed by the Archbishop of Armagh "amid the clang of bucklers and the music of a hundred harps" at **Tullyhogue Fort** (Tulach Óg – "Hillock of the Youths") 3km/2miles from **Cookstown** (signposted on the road to **Stewartstown**). The stone inauguration chair was destroyed by Hugh O'Neill's English pursuers in 1602 and only traces of the fortress remain.

Springhill House at **Moneymore** just across the county boundary in County Derry is one of the prettiest properties managed by the National Trust in Northern Ireland. It was built in the style of a French provincial manor by William Lenox-Conyngham, whose family came to Ireland shortly after the Plantation. The beautifully symmetrical, whitewashed, two-storey building with two "pavilion" wings, is reached by a long avenue with large trees set back from the driveway. The rooms, furniture and artefacts are fascinating; the gardens are lovely. **Springhill Costume Museum** has a particularly fine **Silk Mantua** (a frock worn for formal, royal occasions). There are only 20 of these in the world, and only 7 are fit for display. This one (made in 1759) was worn by several generations of the Clanwilliam family. They were so expensive to make they had to last for ages. (House and museum open weekends and bank holidays June to September 2pm–6pm. Open daily, except Thursdays, July and August 2pm–6pm. Telephone: 028 8674 8210)

A narrow road to the left from the A29 just outside **Moneymore** (Muine Mór – "Great Thicket") will take you to the top of **Slieve Gallion** (528metres/1733ft) for a panoramic view over the countryside over east Tyrone and south Derry.

TOURIST INFORMATION

Omagh Tourist Information Centre, 1 Market Street
Telephone: 028 8224 7831
Cookstown Tourist Information Centre, The Burnavon, Burn Road
Telephone: 028 8676 6727

1 Bushfoot
2 Valley, Portrush
3 Portstewart
4 Castlerock
5 Clandeboye (Bangor)
6 Scrabo (Newtownards)

IRISH SEA

INDEX OF GOLF COURSES

ARDGLASS	156	ENNISCRONE	52
ARKLOW	118	EUROPEAN CLUB	115
ATHLONE	127	FAITHLEGG	105
BALLYCASTLE	9	FERMOY	95
BALLYLIFFEN	25	FINTONA	167
BALTINGLASS	115	FOTA ISLAND	92
BUSHFOOT	10	GALWAY	63
CARNE	51	GLASSON	126
CASTLEGREGORY	74	GLENGARRIFF	82
CASTLEROCK	13	GREENCASTLE	26
CEANN SIBÉAL	73	KENMARE	81
CITY OF DERRY	23	KILKEEL	146
CLANDEBOYE	155	KILLARNEY	74
CONNEMARA (BALLYCONNEELY)	66	KILLYMOON	164
CONNEMARA ISLES	66	KIRKISTOWN CASTLE	156
CORK	91	LAYTOWN & BETTYSTOWN	136
COUNTY LOUTH (BALTRAY)	135	MAHEE ISLAND	158
COUNTY SLIGO (ROSSES POINT)	54	MALLOW	93
CRUIT ISLAND	40	MULLINGAR	124
CUSHENDALL	9	MURVAGH	42
DONERAILE	94	NARIN & PORTNOO	41
DOOKS	76	NEWTOWNSTEWART	166
DOWNPATRICK	157	NORTH WEST (LISFANNON)	24

Otway	37
Oughterard	64
Parknasilla	78
Portrush (Valley)	11
Portsalon	35
Portstewart	12
Rathsallagh	114
Ring of Kerry	79
Rosapenna	37
Rosslare	102
Royal County Down	145
St Helen's Bay	103
St Patrick's Links	39
Scrabo	158
Seapoint	136
Strandhill	54
Tulfarris	113
Warrenpoint	147
Water Rock	96
Waterford Castle	104
Waterville	77
Woodenbridge	117